BARING IT ALL

BARING IT ALL

A MEMOIR

REFLECTIONS OF MY BREAST CANCER ~~JOURNEY~~ F*CKERY

BY AMY BANOCY

YOKE AND ABUNDANCE PRESS
COPYRIGHT © 2023 AMY BANOCY
All rights reserved.

BARING IT ALL: A MEMOIR
*Reflections of My Breast Cancer ~~Journey~~ F*ckery*

ISBN   979-8-88926-600-6   *Paperback*
       979-8-88926-800-0   *Digital Ebook*

To Andrew, Jacob, and Zachary:

Always stay true to you and remember you are capable of doing anything you dream.

CONTENTS

AUTHOR'S NOTE	9
A LOVE LETTER TO MYSELF	19
MAMMOGRAMS (11/12/20–12/10/20)	21
BIOPSIES (12/24/20)	33
THE WAITING (12/24/20–12/30/20)	39
SHIT JUST GOT REAL (12/30/20)	43
CLAUSTROPHOBIA AND SUNFLOWERS (1/5/21)	49
I DIDN'T SEE THAT COMING! (1/6/21)	55
WHAT ABOUT MY KIDS?	63
SUPPORT	69
THEY'RE JUST BOOBS!	75
PLASTICS	81
JOURNAL ENTRY (1/27/21)	89
SURGERY (2/16/21)	91
POST-SURGERY	105
PATHOLOGY (2/25/21–2/26/21)	117
JOURNAL ENTRY (2/26/21)	129
OFFICE OF ONCOLOGY (3/1/21)	131
ALL THE CHEMO PREP	137
CHEMO HERE WE COME (3/16/21–3/17/21)	143
A VERY LONG DAY (3/17/21)	151
THE WEEKS IN BETWEEN	161

HAIR TODAY, GONE TOMORROW	175
CHEMO CONTINUES	185
CHEMO ON MY BIRTHDAY? (4/26/21)	201
A VIRUS AND A BIRTHDAY SURPRISE (4/27/21–5/5/21)	205
SPIRIT (5/8/21–5/19/21)	211
MOVING FORWARD, OR IS IT BACKWARD? (5/19/21)	217
SUPPORT!	225
LAST TC CHEMO (8/3/21)	237
SURGERY NUMBER TWO (9/14/21)	247
CLEAN (9/21/21)	253
RADIATION: THE TECHNICAL SHIT	257
RADIATION: THE EMOTIONAL BURNS (11/3/21–12/14/21)	269
FORGED BY FIRE (12/12/21)	283
THE WONDERING AND TURNING WITHIN (2/10/22)	287
LAST HP TREATMENT (3/30/22)	291
AFTERSHOCK (12/28/21)	297
PHOTOS FROM THE FUCKERY	299
A LOVE LETTER TO MY FAMILY	315
ACKNOWLEDGMENTS	319
APPENDIX	327

AUTHOR'S NOTE

I was a different woman before cancer. One I now know hid behind a facade.

My parents love to tell the story of when I was on the swim team in elementary school. I could easily be spotted in the lap lane, not because of my speedy breaststroke but rather because every time I came up for a breath, I had a huge smile on my face. Throughout my life, I became known for that smile.

I grew up in a safe and loving household, and like most families, we had our struggles too.

While my mom and my sister, Leigh, have a better relationship now, it was very tense when we were growing up. At times there was loud arguing, doors slamming, and words spoken they'd regret. When an argument erupted, my coping mechanism was to escape. I'd run into my room, close the door, face-plant onto my bed, and bury my head under the pillows. The summer before fourth grade we moved to a new house. I can vividly remember turning my closet into my new refuge. I created a "room" in my closet, complete with a sleeping bag, a pillow, a little table and chair, and paper and pens. We made wooden clocks in seventh grade shop class, and mine became part of my closet "room" decor. When the vindictive words began spewing from my mom's and sister's mouths, I hid in this safe haven and scribbled my rage on the page. When they tired of arguing, or slammed enough doors to satisfy themselves, there would be a cease-fire. My dad would talk to my sister and console her. Eventually, he would knock on my door and come check on me. I would smile and say, "I'm fine." I can only imagine what this was all like for him. One daughter wounded by the words of her own mother. The other creating a sanctuary away from the poison. In time, I'd make my way out of the closet to comfort my sister and my mom, each in their own bedrooms.

I continued this pattern into adulthood, albeit without the actual closet. No matter my age and no matter the situation, I'd wait out the storm and smile when it passed, never revealing my true feelings. I smiled because it made me feel safe. I smiled because it hid my pain, my fears, and my tenderness. Being the happy one, the people pleaser, was at times a gift and at times my armor.

Derek and I married in 2001. In 2020 we found ourselves in couples therapy, not for the first time. One of the key things we unearthed was I had built up a wall of resentment over the nineteen years. My lack of understanding how to argue effectively or express feelings I considered "negative," basically anything other than love or happiness, led me to hold all these feelings inside. I didn't want to rock the boat, so I avoided conflict like the plague.

I describe "Before-cancer Amy" as a serial optimist, seldom a worrier, and blissful. My personal and professional life were both imprinted with these traits.

For years, I have practiced the Law of Attraction—manifesting my desires and using the power of positivity to create a fulfilling life. This practice wholeheartedly reinforces my beliefs and supports my outlook on life. In more recent years, I expanded my knowledge through books, TED talks, and online courses. I submersed myself in this work.

I believed in what I was learning and wanted to share it with others. I created and taught a few virtual courses with the mission of helping others cultivate a happiness mind-set and lead a life of abundance. I marketed myself as "The Happiness Guru" and began to book speaking engagements.

My whole world had become about optimism and spreading joy. When challenging situations would arise in my life, or others', I was the one who could find something good in it all. I had the attitude that everything would work out, and worrying was a waste of time. It only infused negative energy into the circumstances.

Why was "Before-cancer Amy" so positive? Was it in my DNA, my genes, or was it something I'd picked up along the way? Was it because I was a people pleaser, peacemaker, and conflict avoider throughout life? Likely, it's a blend of these along with my experiences and perspectives.

I figured I would take all this knowledge and maintain my sunny disposition throughout cancer. Sometimes I did, especially in the beginning. On social media I declared I would "embrace cancer," which meant I'd make the best of the experiences that come with diagnosis and treatment and try to find even the slightest essence of positivity in them. On days when cancer became too much to handle, I promised to remind myself of all I had to be grateful for, find the good even in the bad, and shit like that. I'd convince myself out of the negativity (or so I thought).

As things got crazy and I was hit with unexpected curveballs, I found it hard to keep up the positive mind-set I'd always relied on. This was very difficult for me to grapple with and understand. I then met other women with breast cancer who, like me, struggled with the shame and guilt of not always being happy. They too worried about how not being 100 percent positive might impact their health, and they also didn't have a place to release all their emotions. That is when I knew this book needed to be birthed.

Approximately one in eight women will develop breast cancer in their lifetime (National Breast Cancer Foundation, Inc. 2022).

One in eight!

I heard this statistic many times and never gave it much thought.

I had annual mammograms and never thought twice about what the results might show.

In 2012, I spent the weekend of my thirty-fifth birthday participating in the Avon Breast Cancer Walk. We walked thirty-nine miles over two days and I remember thinking I was walking in support of "other" women. During the opening ceremony they shared a shocking statistic: On average, every two minutes a woman is diagnosed with breast cancer in the

United States (National Breast Cancer Foundation, Inc. 2022). As a way to demonstrate this, a volunteer placed a pink sash on a random walker every two minutes throughout the walk. At the end of the two days, we were able to see how many women had been "diagnosed." I received a sash. I wore it, and still I never thought cancer would happen to me.

I never thought I'd become the one in eight.

I never thought I'd become the "other" I had walked for.

I never thought this would happen to me, just as so many others never think it will happen to them. Yet, here we are.

At age forty-three, in the midst of the COVID-19 pandemic, I was diagnosed with breast cancer and my life flipped upside down. Breast cancer has forever changed me physically, mentally, spiritually, and emotionally.

What follows in this book is my personal story with cancer. You'll notice I do not capitalize the c, as it gives it more undeserved power. I tell it straight, no filters, and I do swear. So if that's not for you, you may want to put this book down right now. (No hard feelings, says the recovering people pleaser.)

Many people refer to their cancer experience as a journey and this has been a journey for sure, a marathon of sorts. Somewhere along the way I began referring to this journey as "cancer fuckery" because, to me, that's exactly what it is. Cancer has fucked with my body and my mind for too long now and I have a feeling, in some ways, it will continue to do so for the rest of my life.

I have a secret—the book in your hands is not the first version of *Baring It All*. I initially wrote a guidebook for women with breast cancer. I was proud of my work and shared it with early readers before it would be printed. Thankfully, a couple of them had the heart and bravery to tell me, "This is good if it's what you want to publish but this isn't what you said you wanted to write." They were correct.

A few days later, while meditating, it occurred to me why I had written that version first. It was my mask, covered in fluff and positivity bullshit with a vibe of, "You got this, girl!" I thought my story wasn't enough to make an impact, and teaching and sharing tips would be the best way to help others. I minimized my worth and my voice and hid behind a costume of serial optimism instead. That guidebook had "Before-cancer Amy" all over it.

Something inside me has always felt that if I took off the mask and revealed deeper emotions, I would lose the way people loved me. They loved my smile, talked about it, and gave me attention for it. I recognized when I felt difficult emotions but couldn't express them, or rather wouldn't allow myself to. Smiling, being happy, and not speaking my truth had always been easier for me.

It was finally time to pull back the curtain and write from my heart.

I wanted to share key experiences, as they are some of the most common in breast cancer. Those include diagnosis, surgery, treatment, and recovery. But most importantly I wanted to talk about emotions. I wrote this book in an attempt to share my story and normalize the full emotional experience of breast cancer.

I have been shocked by the deep range of emotions I have experienced, and continue to experience, as I move through this cancer fuckery. Ranging from some of my most comfortable emotions—such as gratitude, resilience, and strength—to others which felt unusual, uncomfortable, and at times even shameful for me—such as fear, grief, hopelessness, and rage. While to some it may seem logical that one would experience this multitude of emotions, I didn't believe this about myself.

If you landed here as a fellow breast cancer sister, I'm sorry. I'm so fucking sorry. I wish you didn't have to face this disease, and I want you to know you are not alone. My hope is this book provides you comfort, a soft place to land and even a few giggles. I'm glad you are here and we are now in each other's lives. I wish there was a better reason why we now share an initial common bond.

To me, our bond expands far beyond the pages of this book. This book serves as a step toward creating a safe, sacred space for us to honestly feel and express our full range of emotions. While I found emotional support in therapists, counselors, friends, and family, a piece was always missing; none of the people listening and trying to help me had walked this arduous road. Yes, they were able to offer professional and personal support, but many times that wasn't enough for me. I wanted someone who had been through it. Who could relate. Who could truly understand why I was feeling what I was feeling, and not just through a clinical or relational lens.

Baring It All is about more than a book. It is about love, hope, and community.

If you're here as a support person or you are part of a medical team for someone who has cancer, I welcome you and am grateful you're here. While my story may be different than theirs, I am hopeful you will find insights and nuggets that will help you be a beacon of peace and connection as you walk alongside them. Thank you for taking the time to be there for them, in whatever capacity that may be. You may never know just how much it means.

I did not write this book to say there's one way to handle a diagnosis like cancer, or any other major struggle in life. I wrote it because storytelling, raw, vulnerable, and honest in all its moments, is what I do. It's how I process. It's how I function. Most of all, it's how I make an impact. And making an impact is what I want this book to do. If I can help even one woman feel more confident, heard, or loved throughout her cancer experience, I'll consider this a success. If I can help one woman tell her truth or speak up about how she feels, I'll consider this a success.

This book was written in the midst of my cancer fight and a portion of it in the immediate months that followed. Damn, I have such a complex relationship with calling it a "fight." I don't believe anyone "loses" this fight, even when they do not survive. At the same time, I did fight so much through this. I fought this disease, fought emotions, fought with my body, fought with my mind, fought with others, fought insurance companies, fought choices I would make, fought the unfairness of it all, and fought for myself and my life. All that fighting while also trying to make peace with this fuckery and lovingly restore my body.

Breast cancer is complicated and everyone's experience is different. It's something none of us ever wants to face. Yet, we are here. And together, we will grow and endure.

Xo,
Amy

Note: This work depicts actual events in the life of the author as truthfully as recollection permits. While all persons within are actual individuals, names and identifying characteristics of some have been changed to respect their privacy.

A LOVE LETTER TO MYSELF

Journal Entry 1/13/21

Dearest Amy,

I'm writing you today to remind you that, while you may be forty-three years of age, you are not expected to know all the answers. You are being faced with challenges and need to trust and lead from love. Even the oldest, wisest of humans doesn't know all the answers. It is how it is. After all, what would this life be for, if not to learn and grow?

I also want to ask you a big request—that you not be so hard on yourself. You are a beautiful young woman with so many gifts, and I wish you could see yourself as others see you. You have the tools. Turn inward and rely on them as you go through your journey. Think with your heart more than your mind. Trust yourself. Believe in yourself. You are worthy. You are love.

With love and compassion,

Amy

MAMMOGRAMS
(11/12/20–12/10/20)

It's Thursday, November 12, 2020. I sit in a crinkly, paper medical gown, my legs dangling over the edge of the examination table. I look around the exam room and chuckle.

This room never changes.

Monet's paintings hang on the wall; buttons on the ceiling provide women with something to look at when being examined. The nurse left a few minutes ago and now I wait for Dr. Andersen, my ob-gyn, to come in. I'm here for my annual visit, which will include a routine breast exam. Dr. A. has known me since I was thirteen, when I first got my period. She delivered my babies and we have what I consider a special relationship.

Knock knock.

"Yup. Come in," I call.

While we've known each other for thirty years, we've never seen each other during a pandemic. The coronavirus

COVID-19 is in full force. We look at each other with our face masks on. It changes the dynamic when you can't see someone's facial expressions.

I lie back and cringe as she conducts my exam. I stare at the buttons on the ceiling.

"Ok. You're all set Amy. Everything feels fine. You can sit on up and I'll write you the script for your routine mammogram."

We typically chitchat a bit at the end of my appointments. This time, before I sit up, I ask, "Are you sure you didn't feel anything because I've been feeling an extra tenderness in my right breast, similar to how it would feel when I'm about to get my period."

She reexamines me and reassures me that she doesn't feel anything abnormal.

"How's everything else?" she asks as I sit up.

"I'm actually kinda a mess. Things at home haven't been great. Derek and I have been in couples therapy and we were somewhat separated for a short time," I tell her, still sitting on the exam table, wearing only the gown with tears welling up in my eyes.

"Marriage is hard, Amy. So many patients are telling me of marriage troubles, many as a result of being at home together twenty-four-seven since COVID hit. Do you think you guys will be okay?"

I shrug my shoulders, raise my eyebrows, and tell her I really don't know.

We talk for a few more minutes. She bends down, gives me a hug and a few words of encouragement, and leaves the room.

As I change back into my clothes, I feel conflicted. Part of me feels dismissed, having just expressed a strong concern about my right breast, and at the same time I feel loved and cared for because someone I trust told me it was all okay.

Maybe I'm imagining the breast pain. Maybe it's all in my head. I'm sure it's all fine.

These thoughts whirl around like ghosts as I get dressed and leave the office.

Nineteen days later, on December 1, 2020, I arrive at The Radiology Center for my annual mammogram. I check in and answer the typical medical questions, plus a COVID-19 screening. I'm called back to the changing area, where I switch out my shirt and bra for one of those lovely pink medical gowns. The tech walks me to the exam room and, once inside, I place my purse on the chair and stand facing the mammogram machine. The mammographer positions my right breast between the two plates and smooshes it flat like a pancake. She tells me to hold still as she moves behind a glass divider and begins the imaging. She returns and repeats the same with the left breast.

"Did you apply any powder or deodorant this morning?" she asks quizzically.

My body tingles with panic. I've always known not to wear any powder or deodorant to a mammogram because they can show up on the mammogram screening as white spots and can cause inaccurate findings. With a sinking feeling in my belly, I tell her no. She proceeds with the mammogram and I try to suppress my worry.

I've had mammograms since my late thirties, due to having dense, cystic breasts. In all these years, I've never been called for a follow-up mammogram or ultrasound. I've also never had any fear around mammograms. I see them the same as any other routine annual exam and have never given a second thought after leaving an appointment.

A few days after my mammogram, I'm in the kitchen when my cell phone rings. It's a number I don't recognize but something tells me to answer.

"Is this Amy Banocy?"

"Yes."

"Mrs. Banocy, this is Betty at The Radiology Center. We need you to come in for additional mammogram imaging."

My heart sinks. I pull out a chair and sit down. An overwhelming pressure fills my head, like I am going to pass out. I take a deep breath and ask, "Did they see something or did they just not get the images they needed?"

"We just need you to come in, ma'am. I don't know any more than that."

Does this woman not understand how freaked out I am? I mean, I know it's her job to just relay the information and schedule an appointment but this is not an ordinary call for me.

A sinking feeling in my gut tells me something more is going on, yet she can't provide the answers I need to hear. I don't want coldness. I want nurturing, thoughtfulness, and love.

With shaky hands, I put her on speakerphone, so I can look at my calendar. We schedule the appointment for a follow-up mammogram, with the possibility of an ultrasound, for December 10, 2020.

My intuition tells me something isn't right.

Why am I getting called back for a second mammogram? Did they find something? What isn't she allowed to tell me? What if I have breast cancer? I don't get called back for second mammograms.

I end the call and go upstairs to tell my husband Derek. He doesn't seem worried about it, so I tell myself it's probably nothing and try not to think about it too much in the days ahead.

Because of COVID restrictions, I'm not allowed to bring anyone to the appointment. As I sit in the waiting room, I feel unsettled and very alone. I look around the room and wonder what everyone else is here for. Empty chairs, taped off so nobody sits in them, keep us separated at a distance of six feet because of COVID protocols. I scroll through my social media feeds as a distraction, when all I want is someone there to hold my hand.

My name is called and I am taken back to the dressing room to change and then to the mammogram exam room. My left breast is positioned in the mammogram machine. My breathing is heavy and filled with anxiety. She repositions me a few times, as if trying to get it right. She squeezes my left breast flat in between the two cold plates and then moves behind the glass wall to take the images.

It seems like only seconds have passed when she says, "You don't have any powder or deodorant on, correct?"

My heart races, and I breathlessly answer, "No."

Fuck. Shit. She sees something.
But it's my left breast. I had only mentioned the right breast to Dr. A.

After a few more images, she walks me back to the dressing room. I feel like the wind has been knocked out of me. Panic runs through my body. It's hard to breathe.

It can't be breast cancer. It can't be breast cancer.

"You can wait here. Don't get dressed yet. I'm going to show the images to the radiologist and I'll come back to let you know if she wants to do an ultrasound," she says.

I am left alone with my nervous thoughts.

I sit on the small bench and keep the curtain open. My hands fidget and, in an effort to feel some sense of normalcy in the moment, I pick up my phone to respond to a text. I don't even have enough time to do this before she returns.

That was way too quick.

"Go ahead and get dressed. I'm going to take you to meet with the doctor."

With fear coursing through my body, I simply nod, close the curtain, and get dressed.

We walk down the hallway side by side. Perhaps this is a routine occurrence for her.

"Dr. Dallas is one of the best. She's going to take great care of you," she says in a calm and caring voice.

Why would she say that? Why do I need the best unless there's definitely something wrong?

She leads me to a small room, where I sit in one of two plush chairs. I try to hold back my tears while I wait for the doctor. The softness of this room is a stark contrast to other waiting rooms I've been in with their hard plastic chairs. I can't help but wonder if it is a way to make me more comfortable when they relay bad news. I glance to my left and see a glass table lined with pamphlets about navigating breast cancer. My heart beats like a jackhammer in my chest.

A few minutes later, Dr. Dallas walks in. She introduces herself and takes a seat in the other plush chair. The way she looks at me strangely reminds me of how my mom looked at me when I was a teenager and she had to tell me my dear friend had died. I get goose bumps, as I feel the same sadness around the anticipation of hearing devastating news. Suddenly there is a thickness to the air in the room.

"Your mammogram shows several clusters of calcifications on the left breast, none of which were on last year's mammogram. These show up like white spots and look like powder or rice on a mammogram," she says calmly and quietly.

Powder. My instincts had been correct.

"What does that mean?" I jump in, as tears begin forming in my eyes.

She hands me a small box of tissues.

"Calcifications can mean several things. Because there wasn't anything on your mammogram last year and your mom had breast cancer, we want to biopsy two areas to find out more."

"Is it breast cancer?" I ask, my voice now quivering.

"Not necessarily, but we won't know until the biopsies."

My head spins. My stomach churns.

She explains that I will have stereotactic biopsies. This is a type of biopsy which uses mammography to help locate any breast abnormalities and remove a tissue sample for examination under a microscope. During the procedure I'll also have tiny microscopic markers placed inside my breast, to show the areas biopsied.

We schedule the appointment for December 24, 2020. I leave the office in a complete daze.

This can't be happening.

I get in my car and break down crying, filled with fear and with no idea what to do. I've never had to face this type of situation. I can't even think straight.

Do I go home? Do I call my parents? My sister? Derek?
Get it together, Amy. It's going to be okay.

I take several deep breaths and try to figure out what to do next.

I need to tell Derek in person.

My eyes are now puffy and red. I need to let some of this out before getting on the highway to drive home. I decide to FaceTime my mom.

She answers and immediately knows something is wrong. We talk through everything the doctor has told me and she reassures me I'll be okay.

I shake my head and say, "This can't be happening. Mom, I've never had to have a biopsy. What if it's cancer?"

She tries to keep me calm while likely fearful and worried as well. Whenever my mom hears medical news—be it a sore throat, a bad virus, or a shitty mammogram—she tends to have a strong reaction. She fears the worst and goes into management mode. It makes me feel like I now must take care of her and her worries. I get aggravated and my optimism tends to kick in, likely as a defense mechanism. We can't both be worried. One of us must remain positive, and that falls to me.

"Amy, this is so similar to my breast cancer. I had a stereotactic biopsy. It doesn't mean they'll find anything, and if they do, it'll be good they caught it early. I can talk to Karen and find out the name of her breast surgeon."

"Mom. Stop. Please. Hearing all this makes me more anxious. We don't even know it's breast cancer yet."

I need to take this one step at a time. Together, we take a few deep breaths and then I hang up and drive home.

The drive home feels like scenes from a movie are rolling by. I want to hug my boys and tell them I love them. I walk in the door and see Zachary at his desk, head down, as he works on math. I don't want to disturb him, so I quietly walk up behind him, give him a gentle hug and kiss, and whisper, "I love you, bud." He lifts his head and says, "I love you too, Mom. Can we snuggle?" As much as I would love to do just that, I know he needs to stay focused on school and I need to decompress. "Later, bud. I promise."

Andrew and Jacob are both in their online classes, so I will wait to give them love later. As I think about each of my beautiful children, my heart fills with so much love for them and an incredible sense of fear and dread over the situation at hand.

How will this affect them if it's cancer?

I find Derek upstairs in his office and tell him to come into our room and that we need to talk. He tilts his head and furrows his brow.

We sit down on the bed and I begin to sob.

He takes me in his arms, "What is it, Amy? What is it?"

He sounds so scared.

"I might have breast cancer," I mutter between my stuttered breaths.

"What? What did they say at the appointment?" he asks.

With a shakiness in my voice, I relay all the information.

He firmly puts his hands on my shoulders, looks me straight in the eyes, and says, "Amy, we're going to get through this. Whatever it is, we will get through it together."

This makes me cry even harder. This past year hasn't been pretty in our marriage and it overwhelms me to know he will always stand by my side.

I grab a tissue and blow my nose. My eyes meet his as I say, "I feel like this last year of therapy was completely on purpose and for a purpose."

Through his tears, he tells me, "Amy, I'd be here for you no matter what. Even if we weren't together. I love you and I'll always be here for you."

I am so grateful for the work we've done to help us communicate and support each other in our marriage. If this is cancer, we will need each other. I've always been a fan of therapy. I've been in and out of therapists' offices since I was in college and many of those therapists have changed the course of my life. Presently, I am in individual therapy, marriage therapy with Derek, and I participate in group therapy. It is a lot of therapy and, right now, I need it all.

BIOPSIES (12/24/20)

I have shared what's going on with a few close friends and family. My friend Lauren told me she had this type of biopsy, and it had come back as benign (noncancerous). This gives me hope and keeps some of the natural anticipatory anxiety at bay. I am most definitely nervous since I've never had a biopsy, and at the same time, I try to remain positive. I stick to my daily routine as much as possible, perhaps as a way to avoid some of the scarier emotions for me, such as fear and worry. I know being on autopilot is a way our minds protect us, and I definitely need and want a sense of protection.

On December 23, I write in my journal:

Tomorrow morning I will have two areas of my left breast biopsied. I'm certain everything is fine or, at least, it will be.
Everything is figure-out-able.
On the surface I am fine.
Positivity is where I go because it's what I believe.
I honestly know worrying about something can't impact what's already in the cards, so why worry?
But I am worried. I am scared.

I think about the what ifs and don't think it's healthy I'm suppressing all that.
Need to get it out.
Fear thought: What if there's cancer all over my body?
We'll deal with it, and it's not even likely!
Fear thought: What if I have breast cancer?
I'm young and healthy and it's early.
I'm nervous. I'm hopeful. I'm sad. I'm emotional. I'm burdened.

The day of the biopsies is here. I arrive on time, which is unusual for me. All the waiting and uncertainty has been tough to get through. I am ready for some answers. Once again, I have to go alone, due to COVID restrictions. It's traumatizing enough to have to undergo this procedure, and not having anyone here to comfort me before and after is incredibly upsetting. I just want someone to hug me and care for me.

I sit in the uncomfortable waiting room chair and take slow, deep breaths as I wait for my name to be called. I look around the room and wonder what brings each woman here today.

Diagonally across from me, an older woman knits what looks to be a scarf. Every few minutes she readjusts her glasses and repositions them on the bridge of her nose. Three chairs separate me from the woman to my left, who looks to be in her forties and is busy scrolling through her phone. To the other side of me is a cute, stylish young woman, probably in her thirties. She is reading a book and keeps nervously glancing at her watch.

How many of the women here will be told they have breast cancer today? How many are here for routine mammograms? How many are having biopsies like me? Somehow, while we all appear to be different, I find comfort in knowing I may not be alone in this.

My name is called and I feel a sudden chill run the length of my body.

I am really here, about to have this procedure to find out if I have cancer brewing in my body.

I stand up, and with a half smirk, I sheepishly say, "That's me." Even in this moment of fear, I still smile.

But why? Why do I have to hide my emotions?

I may be forty-three years old but in this very moment I am somehow a child again and my smile serves as my shield.

I change into a medical gown and then the nurse leads me to the procedure room. It is bright white and cold. Fluorescent lights glow in the rectangular spaces above. At a quick glance, this could be mistaken for a science lab, equipped for running experiments.

"Amy, when we're ready, you will lie face down on this table. Your breasts will be placed in these two holes on the table. This special mammography machine will take a few X-ray images of your breast, which will later help guide me to the exact area to biopsy today. Once I've located it, I'll numb the area and then insert the biopsy needle and extract the tissue. I'll place the extracted tissue on one of these microscope slides and it will be prepared for the lab. I will then repeat this for the second area to be biopsied today. It is a fairly quick procedure. We want you to be as comfortable as you can throughout this time, so please be sure to tell us if you are in any pain," the radiologist explains.

I stand like a deer in headlights, simply nodding, and so very quietly I mumble, "Okay, okay, yes." I'm not even sure there is any volume to my voice.

After a few minutes, the nurse directs me to lie on the table where the procedure will take place. I lie face down with my breasts hanging through the two holes in the table. As the nurse helps to position me, the radiologist explains that she will slide underneath the table in order to reach the areas of concern and perform the needle biopsies. In my mind, all I can picture is a mechanic sliding underneath a car to perform maintenance. It makes me chuckle to myself, which feels like an emotional release.

"Do you have any questions before we get started, Amy?" she asks.

"No. I'm okay."

Bonnie, the nurse, rubs my back in a reassuring way throughout the entire procedure.

"You're doing great, Amy. Are you comfortable?" her soothing voice asks me.

"Mhm," I manage to eek out.

"We're almost finished with this part."

I want the procedure to be over. I know I have no control over whatever the result will be, and this makes my skin crawl. I clench my fists and do my best to relax, breathe, and remain hopeful my results are benign, just like Lauren's.

An hour later, the procedure is over. Bonnie walks me back to the changing room and gives me small, round, pink ice packs for my breast, along with post-procedure care instructions. I find myself very irritated by their choice of color for the ice packs.

Couldn't they have chosen a different color? Any other color to not have me think about breast cancer?

It is enough I have to be here at all. The color pink makes it all too real and scary for me. It makes me worry and I don't want to. I want to stay positive, but what if those tissue samples she took are ridden with cancer cells?

As I leave the office, I am informed it'll be ten to fourteen days before I'll hear any results. I am so overwhelmed with all that has just taken place, I don't even consider whether this seems like a long time to wait. It washes right over me.

With lumpy, pink ice packs stuffed in my sports bra, I get in my car and drive home.

Damn these ice packs are uncomfortable. Stop it, Amy. It's not the worst thing in the world. Who knows what discomfort you'll experience if this is indeed cancer? Oh my g-d. Cancer.

Suddenly it all hits. My face scrunches up and my cries are loud.

How will I make it through two weeks until I know the results?

I pull into my driveway, wipe the tears, take deep breaths, and silently coach myself to stay positive. I do my best to return to what I know, which is faithful waiting. I trust in my belief that the Universe has a plan for each of us and that whatever may happen, good or bad, isn't happening to us. It's happening for us. Having faith means doing my best to let go and trust. After all, no amount of worry is going to change whatever may or may not be contained on those tissue samples. It is out of my control.

But damn, I pray it is good news.

THE WAITING (12/24/20–12/30/20)

What if I have cancer?
Fuck, fuck, fuck, fuck, fuck.
Why do I feel like it's there? Like I know I have it and I'm just waiting to hear it?
I know it doesn't help to worry, but
Fuck!
How can I not worry?

This is my journal entry on December 28, followed by,

Why the hell do I have to wait for this info? Why can't it be faster?
Because the Universe is on its own time, Amy, and its timing is perfect. If it was too fast, I'd question that too.

Fear and dread not only land in my journal but also overtake my body and my mind.

On December 29, I write:

My mind and body are so anxious.

Tight stomach—literally in knots.
Crying—so emotional.
Wiggly, antsy body—like restless leg all over.
Sweating last night.
Heart racing.
Nauseated.
Headache.
This is the longest fucking week! Don't like feeling all this anxiety. I need it to stop. Need to break this cycle.

I don't want to feel this way.

I want to focus on the positive.

I don't want to sit in these icky feelings and I most certainly don't know what to do with them.

I want to be back in my comfort zone. To turn it all off and be happy, smiley Amy.

I hide all this, though. People ask, "How are you?" and I simply say, "I'm fine." To the outside world, I am still that happy person.

Nothing is good about the waiting. It is agonizing, yet I insist on carrying this heavy burden alone. I am short-tempered with almost everyone and my family catches the worst of my snippy attitude.

Deep breathing, journaling, and meditation are useful practices as they allow these thoughts and feelings to flow out from inside of me. By getting it all out on paper, I am usually able to reframe the narrative running through my mind. I often end these journal entries with gratitude lists. Sometimes this is enough to shift my mood, to provide that little upswing I need to recenter myself.

I am grateful for my family.
I am grateful for my morning writing group (RAW).
I am grateful for people who love me unconditionally.
I am grateful for energy to work.
I am grateful for a quiet morning.

I let my truths out but only in secret. Then I close my journal and pretend.

And at what expense? How much does it cost me to not accept or admit my emotions? How much is it worth to put on the smile?

SHIT JUST GOT REAL (12/30/20)

We all have dates burned in our memory; a wedding, first kiss, special vacation, or death of a loved one. December 30, 2020, is added to my dates as the day I was first diagnosed with breast cancer.

One fateful phone call and my life is forever changed.

"Derek!" I scream as I see Dr. Andersen's name appear on my phone.

He charges into the room like a bull and knows by the look on my face that it is Dr. A.

"I'm so sorry, Amy. Both biopsies came back positive," she relays through the phone.

Words I prepared myself for, words my intuition knew were coming, yet these words still gut me.

Tears begin to fall. I have no control over them. I can't move. I want to get out of this chair, to move my body, but I am stuck.

Derek grabs me a tissue and kneels right beside me, rubbing my leg as we listen and try to take in what she tells us. It is such a sweet gesture, yet I don't want to be touched. I want to run. I want to scream. I want to be somewhere else. Anywhere else.

"It's early stage. DCIS. This means it has not left the ducts, which is great news."

She hears my tears, my sniffling.

"I know, Amy. I am so sorry. It's definitely not what we wanted or ever expected at your age, but we've caught it early and that's so important."

All I can manage is, "Um hmm," to let her know I hear her. I breathe heavily and cry harder. I can taste the salt of my tears.

"At this point, you'll need to see a breast surgeon. I'm going to give you the names of two I recommend. You can meet with one or both. It's up to you."

Up to me? I have no fucking idea what to do! I've never done this before.

I appreciate that she gives me the opportunity to choose. At the same time, it makes my head spin that I have to make such a crucial decision.

How do I choose? What do I look for in a breast surgeon? How will I even know if they're the right choice? What if I choose the wrong one? Why the fuck am I even having to make these decisions? How did this happen to me?

My hand shakes as I scribble down the first surgeon's name and info. She begins to say the second name and I interject.

"Never mind, I'll just call the first one."

The first practice is associated with the same hospital system as most of my existing doctors, so it seems easiest and least overwhelming.

Easiest. That's all I want at this moment. I am flooded. I am emotional. I am in shock.

"This is where I hand you over to the breast surgeon. I won't be involved in the next steps but I'm here. I'm always here for you. Call me anytime. Again, I'm so sorry, Amy. This is one of the worst parts of my job, but I wanted to be the one to tell you rather than some anonymous tech at the radiation center. We go way back, Amy, and I'm here for you."

I end the call and sob heavily into Derek's arms. I can tell he is trying to be strong for me. Trying to hold back his own tears. His own fears.

Here is this man, who only months ago I was thinking of leaving, now comforting me. How could this all be happening?

What the fuck! I have cancer? Oh my g-d. How are we going to survive this? Not the cancer, but what the cancer could do to this marriage we've just barely begun repairing. This is too fucking much.
Focus, Amy. Deep breath.
Focus on the next step.

That's all that's in your control right now.

I know what I have to do. I have to make the next call.

It's early stage. We're going to call a surgeon. She'll do a lumpectomy, just like mom had, and I'll be fine. Just make the call.

I shift into do-whatever-the-fuck-we-have-to-do mode. Survival mode. Perhaps even denial mode?

"Hi. My name is Amy Banocy. Um, I just got a call from my doctor and I had two breast biopsies, which were both positive. She referred me to Dr. Bender for an appointment."

I literally can't believe the words come out of my mouth. It is an out of body experience.

"I'm so sorry, hun. Yes, let me see what we have available. Who's your referring doctor?"

I wonder how many of these calls she's taken. Her warm, calm voice suggests I may be only one of many.

I answer her and we schedule my consultation for January 6, 2021.

I call my parents to let them know the date of my appointment. They inquire about the surgeon and I'm irritated because I know my dad is going to Google her to note her credentials. I shove the feelings aside, as I know he only wants the best for his baby girl and I'm reacting out of being on edge about everything.

"We don't know what to do with ourselves. We kind of look at each other, we cry, and we just feel like we are hanging in midair. We feel helpless being so far away. Are you sure we can't come up?" my mom says with a combination of sadness and guilt in her voice.

"You know I want you here, but I really think it makes the most sense to wait until we have a more concrete plan in place. We're going to need your help," I reply.

We each understand how the other feels. I can only imagine the sheer terror of being the parent in this situation. Once we meet with Dr. Bender and have more information, we can make a plan for my parents to be here.

My little green spiral notebook is filled with questions to ask at our appointment. I have one week to wait.

One week doesn't seem like a long time. Unless you're waiting in angst. Then it feels like time stands still.

CLAUSTROPHOBIA AND SUNFLOWERS (1/5/21)

I need to be alone. I need to process all this. A fucking breast MRI? I can't do it. I can't do this. I need to escape. I feel so stuck in the hurry-up-and-wait process. I just want to go back in time and have this not be my life. I'm exhausted.

While I want to be alone with my thoughts, I am completely enraged that I have to be alone for a breast MRI.

Damn COVID!

January in Northern Virginia tends to be downright cold. Bundled up in my sweater, I yearn to drive with the windows down. I want to feel the fresh air on my face and let the chilled breeze sweep away my anxiety. Instead, the windows are up and the heat is on for the forty-five-minute trip to the MRI center.

Damnit. Why couldn't there be a closer MRI center?

I am beyond overwhelmed with the number of appointments I've been to and now I have this. A long drive seems like such an inconvenience, but it's the closest place able to get me in on such short notice. My stomach is in knots. I look at the other drivers as they pass by and wonder how many are having a routine day. How many are heading to work? Will any of *them* find out more about a cancer diagnosis today?

My mind is like a warped record on its player, stuck in this endless loop of words.

I have cancer in my body.
So many thoughts.
Too many thoughts.
So many appointments.
Oh, my sweet boys.
How will this affect you?
It's just all too much.
Too many questions.
It doesn't serve me to worry or project.
Yet my body experiences the anxiety.
I must get it out.
But how?
Deep breaths, Amy, deep breaths.

I pull into the parking lot and call my sister, Leigh, before I head inside. I need to hear her gentle, supportive voice. My nerves are a bit calmer after we talk, so I take a few more deep breaths, open the car door, put on my face mask, and approach the building. My heart races as I pull open the heavy door. Inside, I sit and wait. My leg nervously shakes up and down. I can hear a constant buzzing noise and find it very annoying.

Why are the chairs in these places always so hard?

"Amy Banocy."

I hear my name and it takes me a minute to snap out of my thoughts to respond. My anxiety is heightening and the nurse walking me back must smell it. She speaks in such a calm tone, like one would when expressing their condolences.

Has someone died? Am I going to die?

As instructed, I change into the gown. I'm beginning to wonder how many of these gowns I'll have to change into during this whole breast cancer fuckery. Like a robot, I simply follow her commands. I sit. I sign consent forms. I put out my arm. I squeeze the red squishy ball she's placed in my fist. I feel a pinch and she has inserted the IV. All the while, she's asking me a series of questions. The answers come out of my mouth but I'm disconnected from them. I am solely focused on my anxiety.

"Amy, have you ever felt claustrophobic?"

That one I fully hear and process. Likely because it registers with what's been occupying my mind.

"Yes! I'm really nervous about that part. I'm very claustrophobic and have high anxiety. I've had MRIs before and it has not been a good experience."

"Okay. That's good to know. This MRI is a bit different and most people seem to tolerate it better since you'll be lying face down on your stomach. How do you feel about that?"

"Still not good, but it is what it is. I just want to get it over with."

She gives me a look that says, "Oh, poor girl."

"Well, let's head down the hall and get you set up."

Following her lead, I try to channel my inner Buddha.

Inhale. Exhale. Inhale. Exhale.

The room is cold and drab.

It would be nice if they brightened up these places. Maybe hung some art on the walls?

I'm so mad I have to even be here and the dreadful room doesn't help any. I glare at the huge MRI machine, which seems to mock me as I look it over.

Everything about the exam is explained to me and I make my way onto the table when instructed. My breasts are manhandled and maneuvered through the holes in the table (similar to the biopsy table), earplugs placed in my ears, and headphones put on. Nothing is comfortable about this experience. And I haven't even slid into the MRI machine yet.

With a gentle voice, the tech asks how I'm doing and if I'm ready to get started, to which I reply, "I'm fine."

Why did I say I'm fine? I am so not fine. I'm fucking miserable right now. My boobs feel like piñatas hanging from a tree branch. I'm cold but sweating. I'm not fine. It's just easier to

say than the alternative. She doesn't REALLY want to know. Or does she?
She's been telling me she wants me to be comfortable. It's her job. Of course she wants me to be honest.

She doesn't make it to the door before I lift my head and abruptly let out, "Wait! I don't think I can do this. I'm so anxious. Can we take a few more minutes?"

We do and she is so compassionate. She offers suggestions such as breathing and meditation during the MRI. I already know these things, and while I know she's only trying to help, I find her suggestions agitate me. I just want to get this over with. I tell her I'm ready and lower my face into the cradle.

She leaves the room and I hear her voice come over the speaker. She tells me she's going to start, but all I can hear is my own breath. It becomes more rapid. My eyes are closed and I try to picture the beach, hear the waves, and imagine myself there. It only makes the anxiety worse. My brain is so twisted right now that trying to think of something different only reminds me of where I am. I am so aggravated by this.

The room feels like it's closing in on me and the only thing that helps is to count and breathe. I count in my head through the entire forty-five-minute scan.

When she returns to the room, I realize I'm crying. I don't know if it's anxiety or relief. All I know is I want out. Now.

I retrace my steps back to the changing room. My hands are shaking so much that I have a hard time opening the locker where my clothes and wallet are stored. After several attempts, I am in. Like a video on rewind, I put my clothes on, just as I'd taken them off.

I grab a tissue and exit the building. I can't stop the crying. I'm trembling as I reach the parking lot.

Damnit I wish someone was here with me. I don't want to be alone, in this parking lot, crying. Filled with fear of the unknowns. What will this MRI show?

I see my car and do a double take. There on the windshield sits a gorgeous bouquet of sunflowers and a card. Before I reach the car, I know who they're from. I get in the car, immediately call my sister, and allow myself to sob the thousands of tears that have been accumulating in my body. In this moment, I am beautifully reminded that, while my sister may not be there holding my hand, I am definitely not alone in this. I'm suddenly overwhelmed with warmth and gratitude.

I DIDN'T SEE THAT COMING!
(1/6/21)

We wake up the next morning, get the kids set up with virtual school, and hit the road for an appointment with the breast surgeon, Dr. Bender. Derek has a meeting afterward, so we drive separately. My eyes are bloodshot and my body exhausted. I wish I didn't have to keep my eyes open. I'm quickly realizing there is no rest for the weary when it comes to cancer.

I'm prepared to hear I'll need a lumpectomy since that's what my mom had when she was diagnosed with a single spot of DCIS in 2016. It will suck yet seems manageable and a simple enough way to ensure cancer will quickly be out of my body and my life.

We arrive and exchange a look and a deep breath before we enter her office. All I can do is shake my head in complete disbelief that we're here. He does the same as he pulls open the front door, and we enter yet another waiting room.

As I fill out the shit ton of paperwork, I glance up at the other women in the waiting room. I appear to be the youngest and healthiest. A deep rage rises from my belly into my throat. I have spent the past eight years making positive changes to my health in an effort to heal autoimmune inflammation, pain, and fatigue. I cut out gluten and dairy; I exercise, do yoga, and meditation; and I've eliminated several stressors in my life, as well as relationships which were no longer serving me. I'd say I am the healthiest I've been in a long, long time.

Cancer does not care I am healthy now! Cancer does not discriminate. I sit here, staring at this health intake form, so fucking mad.

How can I have cancer? How is this even possible?

While enraged, it is also not lost on me that even now, even here, I am comparing myself to others. For a moment I'm back in high school, looking around and noting who's prettier, skinnier, and smarter and wondering why I'm not good enough to be their friend.

Don't cry, Amy. Not now.

In an effort to hold my shit together, I finish the paperwork and walk it back to the front desk. I don't know why I don't want to cry. I mean, of all the places to cry this would be one of them. I am fairly certain they go through a lot of tissues here.

Another woman comes in the front door, and when she sits down, I catch her image in my peripheral vision. She's young.

She's pregnant. Our eyes meet and seem to connect and speak in solidarity.

Oh my g-d. Is she here because of breast cancer?

I feel the rage as it bubbles up again. This time it's for her. It's for her unborn child. How dare cancer wedge itself into the life of an expectant mother! Cancer doesn't fucking discriminate and I hate it.

My name is called and, once again, I snap back to the present moment.

Another exam room. Another nurse. Vitals taken. Medical history reviewed. Another gown to adorn my body. Another uncomfortable chair.

As we wait for Dr. Bender, I fidget nervously with the little green spiral notebook that holds my questions.

She comes in and introduces herself. The first thing I notice is she seems to be around my age, and I wonder how many patients she has treated who are her age or younger.

She's warm, kind, and to the point. She's clinical while also personable, which I appreciate.

"Your MRI does, in fact, show DCIS in the left breast, and unfortunately it is not a single spot. The cancer is vastly widespread throughout your left breast and is very close to, if not in, your nipple."

The tears come quick and heavy. Derek is sitting right next to me and puts his arm around me. Dr. Bender hands me a tissue.

She pulls over the computer to show us the images. A gasp escapes from my mouth. My breast looks like a fucking piece of Swiss cheese with white spots, or holes, to my eye, everywhere.

She speaks clearly and emphatically when she says a lumpectomy is not an option. There is no way to remove all the cancer and save the breast. Should I choose surgery, which is absolutely recommended, a mastectomy is the only choice.

I'm completely devastated. I'm confused. I slump down in the chair, my face filled with a look of defeat.

This isn't how today was supposed to go.

I barely take another breath before I hear her voice again.

"We're also seeing prominent lymph nodes on the left side. There could be some invasive cancer, meaning it has left your breast, but we won't know until surgery. I'll take some lymph nodes and preemptively check them for any cancer."

Mastectomy. They're going to take my breast. My whole breast.

She refers back to the screen.

"The MRI also showed 'suspicious areas' on the right breast. You have the option of a bilateral mastectomy [surgical removal of both breasts]. Based on what I see, I am confident these are not cancerous. However, if you do not want to remove the right breast or you're unsure about it, I highly recommend we biopsy the suspicious areas, just to make sure."

It is an MRI biopsy, which means being back in an MRI machine. There is no way I want to get back into that machine again! But the other option is to choose to lose the right breast too, or leave it with suspicious areas.

How am I supposed to make these life-changing decisions?

The spiral bindings of my notebook have created indentations in my hand. I've been clutching it tightly for nearly an hour. I open my notebook and, as I glance through my list, I realize she's addressed all of our questions. I want some clarifications, though, so I ask her to repeat some of the information she's shared, and I numbly nod through most of it. Derek leans forward in his chair, listening, taking it all in.

I wonder what he's thinking. His wife has cancer. His wife is going to lose at least one breast and has to decide whether or not to keep the other.

"I know this is a lot for both of you to digest. I'm going to walk you down the hall to meet with Jane, my surgical coordinator. While we've been talking, she's been working with your insurance and scheduled some of the next appointments you'll need, including genetic testing and the plastic surgeon. She's great and will be a huge help to you. Most importantly, you're going to be okay, Amy. We're going to take very good care of you. Do either of you have any other questions?"

We shake our heads and look at each other for confirmation. We're both completely stone-faced. Dr. Bender leaves and my hands tremble as I remove the gown and change into my clothes.

After almost three hours, we leave Dr. Bender's office and walk in silence to my car. In addition to my little green notebook, I now hold a list of appointments scheduled for me and a book about breast cancer—that seems larger than any book I'd ever open. When Jane handed the book to me, she chuckled and called it the "Bible of Breast Cancer."

When we get to my car, Derek looks me in the eyes and gives me a tender hug. I'm not sure who it serves more, him or me.

Does this feel as awkward for him as it does for me? I appreciate the hug. It's comforting, yet until recently we haven't been intimate. I want to get in the car and break down to my parents and sister.

I release myself from his arms and get in my car. Through my tears, I watch him walk to his car and drive away. I know I don't have energy to relay this shit twice, but I desperately want to be held by my parents and my sister. I FaceTime them together and sit in the parking lot for another thirty minutes, staring at their faces, as I share this devastating news. My mom has tears in her eyes and her hand up to her gaping mouth. My sister is stoic and I can see the pronounced horizontal wrinkles on my dad's forehead. They are shocked. They are upset. My parents want to come up to Virginia from Florida. They have questions I don't have answers to. I am irritated. I don't have energy for questions. I just want them to hold space for me. I'm beyond exhausted. I decide I need time alone with my mind. I need to process. I need to escape. I end the call on a loving note, wipe the tears from my eyes, and begin the drive home. When I pull into the driveway, I can't even remember how I got home. My eyes are filled with tears and I wonder how I will walk into this house and look into the eyes of my children.

WHAT ABOUT MY KIDS?

No mother wants to tell her children she has cancer. Knowing I have to share this news with my boys is absolutely gut-wrenching. I'm not even sure how much they know about cancer.

They know my mom had breast cancer several years ago and my dad had both prostate and kidney cancer. They know both are now healthy and well. Have they seen cancer scenes in movies or TV? These days, the entire world is at their fingertips. How will this news impact them? We don't keep secrets here. How will they react based on the tension that's already been in the house over the past several months?

Only a few months ago we sat the boys down to talk with them about the state of our marriage. While we didn't share all the details, it was a challenging, emotional conversation. At the time I craved independence and space. Our therapist recommended we try to create this while both remaining in the house rather than one of us moving out. We shared that Derek would sleep in the basement and I in our bedroom.

Which news is scarier for them? Derek and I having challenges or their mom having cancer?

I never anticipated I'd sit the boys down for another tough conversation again so soon. Between the COVID-19 pandemic, virtual schooling, all five of us in the house all the time, and our splintered marriage, these boys have been through enough in the past year.

I sit on my bed, my head in my hands, and weep while thoughts continue to rule my mind.

My job is to protect them, not scare them. I don't want to tell them!
Should we tell them all together or individually? They process information differently and will have varied emotional responses. And the age and maturity gaps (Zachary: seven; Jacob: twelve; Andrew: sixteen)?
Just how much do we tell them? How should that vary based on their age and ability to handle this information?
How will they each react? How do we respond to their reactions? Shit! Fuck! I don't want to do this!

Before I had my biopsies, Derek and I reduced that story to its bare bones. We had told the older boys that the doctor found things she wanted to further check in my breast, so I'd have a minor procedure for her to do that. We made it age appropriate for Zachary and told him I was having a little procedure and he'd need to be careful when hugging me. They were mostly unfazed. We didn't anticipate what lay ahead and the arduous conversations to come.

The weight is too much for a parent to bear.

I have to tell them I have breast cancer. Breast cancer.

An unsettled feeling lands in my belly and makes me shake my head. I don't want to rock their world this way. I recognize the delicate balance between them knowing and understanding what is happening and not making them incredibly fearful.

We decide to tell Andrew and Jacob together and talk with Zachary separately.

I stay in our bedroom while Derek goes downstairs to tell the older boys we need to talk with them upstairs. They always know it's serious when we tell them that so, of course, they enter our room with their guards up. I can feel the stiff heat in the room.

Do they think we're about to tell them we're getting a divorce? Will this seem lighter or heavier than if it were that? I don't want them to worry about me. I'm supposed to be the one taking care of them, not the other way around.

This thought runs deep within me, as it's a sticky place in my relationship with my own parents. Therapy helped me realize it's a place of deep resentment from the days of being the one to make my home peaceful again after my mom and sister's fights. I was a child, yet my role was to take care of others and I accomplished the task. In doing so, everyone assumed I was okay, when in fact I was crushed.

I will not let cancer repeat this pattern with my own children.

I take a deep breath and look at Derek, who nods and gives me a compassionate smile conveying his support and confidence in me. I look at my boys and slowly say, "So, you know how I told you the doctors saw some things they didn't like in my breast and they were doing the biopsies? Well, they've looked at it further and…"

The tears come.

I want to be strong but I am so scared. I am numb and my insides tingle with trepidation.

Breathe, Amy, breathe.

"…and it's cancerous. The good news is they caught it early and the doctors are confident that, with surgery, they can get all of it out."

I explain to them the difference between a lumpectomy (and remind them that's what Nanny—my mom—had) and a mastectomy.

"I will have a bilateral mastectomy, which means they will…"

More tears emerge from my eyes. Lots of tears. The moment hits me hard and it is suddenly all too real. This cannot be happening!

But it is. Right here, in my bedroom, on my bed, as my boys sit next to me and Derek.

"I will lose both of my breasts…"

"I'm sorry," I say. I don't know why I apologize for crying.

"It's okay, Mom," they both say in a hushed tone. Andrew shifts back and forth uncomfortably. They each try to console me in their own sweet, childlike way. It's the only way they know how, yet I can see the worry in their eyes.

I don't want to overwhelm them, so I only share a little more about the surgery and what to expect during my recovery.

Neither of my boys are big talkers. Andrew is a processor and I know he needs to sit with this information. He says nothing. This doesn't alarm me since at times he's filled with emotion and other times his emotions are enigmatic.

Jacob tends to be more open with his feelings, so it doesn't surprise me when he says, "Did you know breast cancer is the most curable of all the cancers? I learned about it in health class. You're going to be okay, Mom!" I hug and thank him.

I ask if they have any questions and they both shake their heads. Andrew seems anxious to get away from the situation. He asks if they can leave the room. I nod. They walk out and I melt into Derek's arms in a puddle of tears.

A couple of days before the surgery I tell Zachary I'll be having a procedure and Nanny and Papa are going to be here to help us out. I mostly focus on what to expect during my recovery. The conversation is straightforward—less emotional and more vague than with his brothers. The word cancer isn't even spoken.

Should I have told them more? Less?
They said they were fine, but are they really?

How will all this affect them?
How will I be a good mom throughout all this?
Was it better to show my emotions and tears or should I have kept them to myself?
My boys! My sweet, sweet boys! Will they ever be the same after this?

SUPPORT

In the days that follow I am absolutely exhausted and mentally drained, like I've run several marathons back to back. I know I need to take care of myself and also want to share the news of my surgery with close friends and family, especially those who knew about my mammograms and biopsies. I simply can't reach out to everyone and have a personal conversation, or I will shrivel. I ask my mom and sister to share the news with some family members. I immediately receive text messages of love and support. I appreciate that people know not to call, as it will overwhelm me.

I want to personally update a few close friends, including Layton, Courtney, Lauren, and Jen, who are integral people in my life. I want to call them but do not have the energy, and I know they completely understand. I text them and they each respond in their own loving way, offering their ear when I am ready to talk and their arms anytime I want a hug. Friends like them certainly make life more secure, safer.

I share updates with my therapy group, which consists of my therapist Martha, her co-therapist John, and five other participants. They've all been together for over a year and I am the newbie, just a few months in. I knew it would take time to connect with the group and that just hasn't happened yet.

It doesn't help that, because of COVID, our meetings take place virtually, which creates a different energy. I feel like teenage Amy, trying to fit in. The times when I've spoken up, I've felt like "too much." When silent, I've questioned whether to assert my thoughts. Various people have responded in ways that should've felt comforting, yet I still question my place in the group.

"I want to hear from you, Amy."

"I really like having you in the group. I want to get to know you better."

"You have to be completely honest here."

Perhaps this struggle to fit in as my true self is something I can work on here. Maybe it's part of the process.

Sharing that I have been diagnosed with cancer feels like I've dumped a boulder on the group. I don't know their personalities well enough to read their reactions.

I see the shock on their faces. Is this too much for them to handle? I inserted myself in this group to find help for my marriage, not cancer support.

I feel a completely different energy when I tell my RAW sisters about my diagnosis. They immediately offer to support me in any way possible. I love these women because they are warm, loving, kind, and introspective. The looks on their faces may be the same as those in my group therapy, but I know they will hold space for me and I won't be "too much" for them.

I have been attending RAW (Re-Awakening Wisdom Daily) for about six months. Almost daily, for an hour each morning, I meet with the group virtually. During the first thirty minutes of the hour, we journal and then Alisha, our facilitator, opens the meeting up for discussion. The collective wisdom of these sessions has helped me deepen my spiritual practice and I thrive on the aspects of community, creativity, and continued growth.

Some of the things I love most about RAW is how we speak our truths with zero judgment and no advice is offered unless requested. This alone makes it easier for me to open up here than with my therapy group.

When I started attending RAW, I had no idea the way in which these women would care for me, hold me, and carry me through the isolation of COVID-19, marriage matters, and a cancer diagnosis.

Later in the day I sit down at the computer to send a single email to a group of women I've grown apart from in recent years, but with whom I share a lot of history. We raised kids together, traveled together, practiced Judaism together, and were a team when one had breast cancer several years ago. I hope they are able to put the recent distance behind and show me the same love and support we all gifted Debbie when she had cancer. Because of our shared history, I feel they deserve to know about my diagnosis before I share it more publicly, but I'm still nervous.

My hands tremble as they hover over the keyboard and my heart pounds out of my chest.

Amy, these women love you. You've known them for years and have been through so much together, including cancer. Stop overthinking this.

I begin the email by sharing my breast cancer diagnosis, and I also take the opportunity to disclose what I've kept private.

"Derek and I have been in very intense therapy, working on our relationship and marriage. Over the course of this time in therapy, we've had conversations of separation, divorce, and all the things, and it's been a whirlwind of a year to say the least. We are thankfully in a much better place now, which I am so grateful for. That said, it is still shaky around here, but I am so grateful we are where we are and have done the work of the past year before this huge curveball was thrown our way. I can't imagine the additional stress otherwise!"

Do not delete this, Amy. Press send now. There's a reason you want these women to know what is happening in your life.

With the click of a button—and an exhale of "Shit!"—my words are off to them. I am relieved when I receive their email responses, each woman offering care and support. A part of me also questions whether their offers will hold, in spite of the distance that has grown between us. There has been a clear separation of "me" and "them" and it leaves me wondering how this distance might impact this chapter of our story.

Will cancer bring us back together? Will it create a larger gap? Will they show up for me?

Once I have informed those closest to me, I decide to share more publicly through social media.

The response is overwhelming. Hundreds of people I've known from all walks of my life comment and provide love and uplifting words.

"Love you, Amy! I know you will tackle this just like you tackle everything—like a *beast*! Prayers for healing."

"Sending you so much love, strength, and prayers. I know you will lead the way through this with grace and positivity."

"Sending you lots of love, Amy! Cancer does not discriminate but it sure as shit picked the wrong chick! I know you will come through this experience stronger and wiser…just like you do with everything that comes your way. Please let me know if you need anything. xo"

"Thank you for sharing. Sending healing thoughts your way! And making my appointment this week! Thank you for the reminder on that too."

I receive an abundance of emails, cards, flowers, and gifts.

I am not alone. I have community. I am so blessed.

THEY'RE JUST BOOBS!

I developed breasts at a young age and they grew quite fast. I don't remember ever wearing a training bra. I was the girl everyone said "developed overnight." By the time I was in high school, I wore a D cup minimizer bra. While many girls flaunted their growing chests, as a symbol of womanhood and sexuality, I tried to hide mine. I wore clothes that hid my breasts and stood hunched over to try and minimize them.

"You're so lucky to have such big boobs, Amy."

"All the guys always look at your chest, Amy."

"If you've got 'em, flaunt 'em, Amy."

I heard words like these from my peers on repeat and absolutely hated it. It made me feel as if all the other qualities about me—my personality, my intelligence, and my internal beauty— weren't seen and probably didn't matter.

I started to resent my body. I hated my boobs. It seemed they were the only thing people saw when they looked at me. And since they were the largest part of me, I began to define my entire body by my boobs. This led to a hatred of my body and this body image issue stuck with me into adulthood.

When I was pregnant and later delivered my first child in 2004, my boobs had become absolutely massive. So massive, someone actually made the poor choice of telling me they "look like Christmas hams!"

Talk about salt in the wound.

As I breastfed my son, I found myself completely fearful that I might suffocate him.

I'd always said that if faced with breast cancer, I would confidently say, "Just take them. They're just boobs." That is until now, when I actually have to make this decision.

Thoughts whirl around in my mind:

If I keep the right breast, will I constantly worry about getting cancer there?
Why would I remove a breast that doesn't have to be taken from me?
I have no genetic markers for cancer, so is it really likely there is cancer in the right breast or ever would be?
Why put myself through more biopsies when I can just remove it and have peace of mind?

They are more than just boobs. They are *my* boobs and I am more attached to them than I ever realized. Logically, I know they can be replaced. But that doesn't change the fact that these, these boobs here, are mine.

I grew them.

And at the age of forty-three, not long before cancer invaded, I had just started to love them.

In recent years, I've done a lot of work with my therapist to help improve my body image and become more comfortable with my sexuality. Much of this improvement came down to a realization and belief that my breasts are a beautiful part of me and only I control the narrative around my body. I have finally accepted that it is healthy to experience pleasure, especially as it pertains to my breasts. How is it that now, after all that work, I may lose them both?

Since cancer invaded my life, I've had to make many decisions, some easier than others and many I never imagined I'd have to make. And I've made several decisions that differed from any thoughts or plans I'd always believed I would make when facing such a situation. I have learned more about breast cancer, genetics, and plastic surgery than I ever may have wanted. I rely on that knowledge, plus my own intuition and inner wisdom, to help guide me now. I meditate and try my best to let go of fear. It's so difficult.

I am enough. I am a strong and grounded human. I am more than my body.

In these moments of reflection, I am grateful to have spent the past five years on a deeper spiritual journey. I try to remind myself that life happens on purpose and for a purpose, even if it makes zero sense in the moment.

I simply can't come to terms with the risks of leaving the right breast intact. I will have a bilateral mastectomy.

I will lose both my breasts.

The irony is not lost on me—that I have only recently begun to truly love and respect my body, and now significant parts of it will be taken away and new parts given. I know I will face challenges and for those I am prepared as much as I can be. I make a promise to love this body and to honor this body. Now and in its future state.

Will I be able to keep this promise?

While I feel this is the right decision for my health, I do not welcome it.

I cry and tell Derek, "It's not fair. I finally started accepting my body and now it's being taken from me and changed!"

No woman should have to make this decision. These breasts have fed all three of my babies and I had to decide whether to keep one of them.

I am so mad at cancer.
I am mad at my body for betraying me.
I am sad that I will be losing my breasts.
I am pissed that our patriarchal society makes it seem like no big deal.

I am envious that other women in my life will still have their breasts.

Well, I guess there is one consolation. I get to choose my new boobies! Smaller and perkier? Yes please.

PLASTICS

Life is beginning to feel a bit like Groundhog Day. Today we have an initial consultation with the plastic surgeon, Dr. Mann. Since deciding on the bilateral mastectomy, I've researched possible reconstruction options. I never thought I'd search "breast cancer reconstruction" on Google. I get so mad at the reality of it all that I cry and slam the computer shut.

Implants? DIEP flap? Flat? Too much to weigh. Pros and cons to each. I shouldn't have to be making these decisions.

Based on what I've learned, I'd prefer to have the DIEP (Deep Inferior Epigastric Perforator) flap surgery. From what I understand, this is when they make an incision in the lower abdomen and use tissue from this area to create new breasts. It avoids the need for implants.

Since sharing my diagnosis on social media, as well as that I will undergo a bilateral mastectomy, several people have reached out with either their own breast cancer story or that of someone they know. The most impactful messages have been from women who've had a mastectomy. They've graciously shared tips for surgery and recovery as well as their personal experience with implants or DIEP flap surgery.

Knowing I'm not alone is comforting but the messages have also become overwhelming. I can barely keep my head above water most days and the plethora of messages makes me submerge once again.

I know they're trying to help. I've always leaned on others in making decisions, but I know I need to get quiet and make this life changing decision on my own.

Amy, where does your intuition guide you?

We enter Dr. Mann's office and it feels so Beverly Hills. I have never been in a plastic surgeon's office and it's exactly as I imagined it. Bright lights. Nice couches and chairs in the waiting room. A glass cabinet filled with overpriced, fancy products. Frames displaying information about cosmetic surgeries and injections. I sigh and roll my eyes.

I feel so out of place. People come here because they choose to have cosmetic surgery. I'm here because cancer forces me to be. How is this fair?

I approach the front desk and tell them my name. My body is tight and I'm sure my attitude is snarky. I'm given a clipboard with several papers to fill out. I sit down in one of the plush chairs and complete the forms. Some seem necessary. Others irritate me, as it's repeat information I've already shared with Dr. Bender.

This is so annoying. Why can't they make this easier? I'm an emotional wreck and do not have the patience to do this shit over and over.

Despite my annoyance with the situation, I begrudgingly complete the forms and return them to the woman at the front desk.

I wonder how old she is and if she's had plastic surgery or injections. Her face looks taut yet her hands are wrinkled. Why do I care? Why am I thinking about this shit right now. I wonder if she feels sorry for me since I'm not here by choice?

I return to my seat and we're soon called back to the exam room. I carry with me my bag, a bottle of water, and my trusty green notebook. I'm self-conscious and fidget with it.

Will he think I'm insulting his expertise with all these questions?

I feel like a little girl, not the grown ass woman I know I am.

The nurse hands me a gown to change into and I return to the present moment.

Yes, I am a woman who knows what is best for her! I will ask my questions, voice my concerns, and be confident. I don't want implants. I want to use my own body tissue. I don't want those foreign objects in my body. I don't want to be a "plastics." It's just not me.

I realize I've just equated implants to vanity.

I take the gown and immediately notice this one is different than the others I've worn as of late. It's soft. It's long. It's a relaxing blue. I put it on and it feels like a robe from a spa.

Wouldn't that be nice? I'd much rather be there than here. That's for damn sure.

I take a seat on the edge of the exam table. The lovely, standard, paper lining rustles beneath me.

I'm most definitely not at a spa!

Derek sits in a chair directly across from me. He looks incredibly nervous. I'm so grateful I'm allowed to bring someone with me today. With where Derek and I have been in our relationship, it's also awkward he's here with me to help me make decisions about the fate of my breasts. Breasts I haven't desired him to touch in months.

I glance behind me and see a row of implants lined up on the windowsill. I try to break the thickness in the air.

"It's a boobie buffet."

We both chuckle. It's obvious we're laughing out of fear and discomfort more than humor.

Dr. Mann comes in and our laughter stops. He spends some time discussing what he knows of my case. He is kindhearted and comforting. I immediately like him and am glad I chose him as my surgeon. He makes me feel like an actual person, not just another patient on his schedule. All this helps me feel more at ease about my little green notebook. He sits down on the swivel stool and begins talking about reconstruction.

"There are a few different options for reconstruction. The first is breast implants. At the time of surgery, after Dr. Bender has removed the breasts, breast tissue, and any lymph nodes she needs, I will place tissue expanders in place of the breasts."

He picks up what looks like a tiny plastic frisbee and extends his hand toward me. I awkwardly hold it as he explains to us how he will fill this tissue expander with saline over the weeks following surgery. This will allow for the chest wall to expand and make room to accommodate the implant, which will then be placed during a second surgery. The tissue expander is somewhat flimsy and flexible but the edges are rigid, as they are metal. I can't imagine this being in my body. I listen to him, but my defenses are already up.

I don't want those fake things in my body.

"I don't want implants," I pipe up and boldly state.

He kindly asks what my concerns are and I take the opportunity to state my case.

"Well, I already have autoimmune diseases and I don't want a foreign object in my body. It scares me to think my body might reject it, which would then lead to additional medical issues."

Dr. Mann leans in and I take a deep breath, wondering how he will react to my next thought.

"I also have a couple of friends who've had their implants removed [explanted] because of symptoms related to breast implant illness. I just don't want to go that route. I want to use my own body tissue for reconstruction."

I choke up. I'm not sure if it's the part of me that always feels timid speaking my voice or if it's simply because we're even here, having this conversation with a plastic surgeon.

He hands me a box of tissues and lends some insight and opinions. I'm still not convinced implants are for me, so I tell him I want to hear about the DIEP flap surgery option.

He asks me to stand up so he can look at my belly and evaluate whether I have the necessary amount of tissue for this surgery. I feel so vulnerable, standing here, my gown pulled open, while he examines my body. I look down at my post-baby belly and wait for him to tell me that he'll easily be able to make new boobs out of it and that I won't need implants.

His eyes meet mine.

"I'm sorry Amy, but you don't have enough fatty tissue in your belly. Sometimes we use the inner thighs, but you don't have enough there either. I just don't know that DIEP is really an option for you."

Are you fucking kidding me? Not only do I have breast cancer and have to deal with this shit, but now I'm basically being penalized for my healthy body? This is absolutely maddening! This belly that I squeeze and hate isn't fatty enough? Oh, the irony of it all.

"What do you mean I don't have enough?"

He explains that there's probably enough fatty tissue in my abdomen to make A cup breasts. I am 5′7″ and 155 pounds so, no, an A cup won't look proportional on my body. And while I'd love smaller boobs than what I have now, going from an E to an A just isn't it for me. I want a C cup.

I appreciate how much Dr. Mann understands my points and my hesitations. He addresses every question I have in my notebook and those that have come to mind throughout the appointment. We talk through some additional information about the breast implants, as it seems this is likely the surgery I'll have at this point.

"I know this isn't what you expected to hear today. I want to make sure you are happy with the end result, so please don't hesitate to ask me any questions between now and the surgery date. You're not the only one I've had to have this conversation with and it's never easy. You're going to look great, Amy."

Despite his care, I am uncomfortable sitting here. I continuously adjust the front of the gown to be sure my breasts are covered. My feet are fidgety as they dangle over the edge of the exam table.

A familiar thought once again passes through my mind: *How the fuck is this my reality?*

Dr. Mann leaves the room. Derek hands me my clothes and I get dressed. He knows I'm upset and disappointed. We are walked down the hall to the surgery coordinator's office where we review details for surgery and she assures me I will be happy with my implants and that Dr. M is the best. I'm annoyed because she looks like she's had a "boob job" for fun, and I do not want those things in my body. I also don't want a flat closure and to have no breasts at this age and stage in my life.

Her words are like background noise. I'm thankful Derek is here and hopeful he takes in a bit more of this than I am right now. She hands me a folder filled with information about surgery, implants, and recovery. She excitedly shares a voucher with me.

"This is for you to come back and get a free facial once you're recovered."

Well, isn't that a nice touch?

"I'll definitely take you up on that! I'll be back for sure!"

My bilateral mastectomy with tissue expander placement is scheduled for February 16, 2021.

I have less than three weeks left with my current body. I will continue to prepare mentally, emotionally, and physically for this next leg of my fuckery. I pray that along with losing my breasts I will also lose all the cancer.

JOURNAL ENTRY (1/27/21)

I am protected and safe.
I have my breath.
I am being held.
I am being guided.
This is all my unique journey.
There need not be stress or resistance; simply what is is, and go from there.
I am protected.
I am loved. I am love. I am breath.
I am divine.
I am divinely guided.
I am breath.
Lessons will be learned.
Much like all of life.
We learn to do.
We've always had our breath.
Return to that.
Stop doing.
Start and keep breathing, being.
It is all part of the journey.

My journey.
I am learning.
Trust what you learn.
Be divinely guided.
Trust.
Know.
Be.
Breathe.

SURGERY (2/16/21)

It's three days before surgery and my parents have arrived. They've traveled nearly twenty hours overnight on the auto train from Florida. Because of COVID-19 restrictions, we haven't seen each other in over a year, which is very atypical. One of my neighbors, who is also a close friend, has been living and working remotely in Florida for several months as a perk of COVID restrictions, which keep her from the office. She generously offered for my parents to stay in her house and make it their home while they're here. This will enable my parents to come over at a moment's notice, to not have to pay for a hotel or rental during this extended stay, to have a place to do their laundry and eat their meals, and to walk across the street and take a rest when needed. She has given us the greatest gift!

Their car pulls into the driveway and Zachary jumps up from the couch with elation. I don't think he really understands why they're here, though. We run downstairs, open the garage, and Zachary runs right up to the edge as it opens. It's raining, as if the sky is shedding tears for us.

Are they tears of joy that we can be together or sadness as to the reason why?

As soon as they enter the garage, Zachary reads a poem he wrote:

"My poem for Nanny and Papa.
*Roses are red,
Violets are blue.
I have never met anyone,
as loving as you.*"

My mom cries and pulls him into a giant hug followed by hugs from my dad. I record this special moment on my phone. Mostly to have the memory but also because I know the focus doesn't have to be on me as long as I allow it to remain on Zachary. As soon as she makes eye contact with me, I know my mom is silently telling me all the feelings she's felt since our FaceTime call after my mammogram. And when either of my parents hug me, I know I will feel my sadness and fear untangle and become surrounded by their own.

Our eyes lock and we hug. In their embrace, I realize just how much I need my mom and dad right now. Tears begin to fall, and I shake them back in an effort to protect Zachary from any worry. The sweet innocence and juxtaposition are not lost on me: that he was so happy to see them yet cannot fully understand why they are here. This visit won't be like others.

As we close in on my surgery date, I feel very overwhelmed. There is so much to buy, to clean, and to take care of before this surgery. As the mom, I feel like the CEO of the Banocy household. I hold the golden keys to the kids' plans, school information, friends' contact info, etc. Derek is an involved dad, but I have always taken care of these things. Perhaps it's part of my control issue? Call it whatever you want, but it leaves me anxious and unsettled to know I will be out of commission for weeks. My stomach turns over like choppy waves in the ocean. My arms and legs squirm as I try to escape the tension.

I bring all this up in group therapy and my therapist, Martha, suggests I pass some of the responsibilities on to others. This is a foreign concept. I do not like to ask for help. In fact, the thought of delegating some of these tasks makes the waves in my stomach roll faster and my chest tighten.

What if it's not done the way I want?
What if it doesn't get done at all?

The next day our fucking dishwasher breaks! I am a healthy woman, diagnosed with breast cancer in the midst of a pandemic, about to lose my boobs. The dishwasher is the straw that breaks the camel's back and I know I need assistance!

It is time to listen to Martha and bring in the reinforcements. I simply can't do it all. I feel like a child when I ask my mom to order the things I may need post-surgery and ask Derek to please order a new dishwasher. They of course jump in and do what is needed. I am no longer the child. I am a strong woman, capable of asking for help.

Mom orders post-mastectomy bras, a shower stool as I will be too weak to stand for some time, and button-down shirts because I won't be able to lift my arms for probably four to six weeks. All these items have come as suggestions from women who have had a mastectomy. And, thank goodness, Derek orders and installs a new dishwasher.

As each thing gets checked off the list, a weight lifts off my shoulders. I realize now that asking for help is not the weakness. To not ask for help would be the weakness because I would overload and this would cause stress, which my body certainly does not need. While it was hard to do and it left a sourness of sucking on a lemon in my mouth, I had to let myself be helped.

With my parents in town, Derek and I are even able to get away for a couple of nights before surgery. We head to a cabin in the mountains. Somewhere quiet. Somewhere isolated from reality.

I had read about women who had pictures taken or sketched before their mastectomy, and I thought this sounded like a great way to remember and honor the loss of my breasts. And since Derek is an artist, it was an even better idea. Before going to the cabin, I shared the idea with Derek, and asked him to sketch my body. I felt so incredibly vulnerable. I mean, yes, he's my husband but I'm not one to pose nude, even for him! He told me he'd heard this idea too and was going to ask if I wanted to do it.

All weekend I keep putting it off. The last night we are away, I say, "Okay. As weird as this may feel now, I know I am going to want these sketches later, so let's do it." He encourages me to relax, and while it is awkward for me as it's not something

I've done before, we have some laughs, and the drawings turn out just as I'd wanted.

I'm losing the shape of my body as I know it. A body I have worked so long to be comfortable living inside.

I reflect back and wonder why over the years I'd heard and even said, "Oh, they're just boobs!" so flippantly? We don't say "Oh, it's just a penis!" or "Oh, it's just your kidney! You have another one." So why boobs? Do we disrespect breasts so much that we're quick to think we'd just as easily lose them, rather than see if there's a way to keep them?

It's the night before my bilateral mastectomy. I am both ready and restless. I focus on entering this surgery with a positive mind-set.

I've received numerous messages today offering ease and healing as I head into this life-altering surgery.

One message is from my friend Lauren. She and I initially met through doing business together almost a decade ago and formed a deep bond over the years.

"I am covering you in love and light and prayers. I cherish your friendship and the joy you bring into the world. Take that with you into surgery tomorrow. I love you!"

Friends, family, sorority sisters, my RAW sisters, and acquaintances I haven't seen in decades have volunteered to bring meals to my family for several weeks after my surgery. I am overwhelmed with gratitude for my incredible community.

"Amy, you've spent your life cultivating these relationships and being there for others. Now it's your time to receive," Derek sweetly tells me.

Derek and I have to be at the hospital at 6:30 a.m. My bag is packed with a front closure post-mastectomy bra and a button-down post-mastectomy shirt since I won't be able to lift my arms to put on regular clothes. I've been told by the doctors that I may not be able to do so for another six weeks! It feels like postpartum healing all over again. My bag also holds essential oils, my journal, pens, and phone charger, as well as the beautiful mala beads my friend Kate gave me and some of my favorite healing crystals. I'm not sure any of this will even make it out of my bag, but knowing they are close by helps create an energetic space for healing.

My sweet friend Rebecca, who I met through RAW, offered to do distance Reiki for me. We'll do it right before bed, so I can fall asleep wrapped in her healing energy.

I lay my head on the pillow, listen to Rebecca's peaceful, calm voice in my ear, breathe deeply, and try my best to put my nerves to rest and fall asleep.

I wake up with a stroke of fear and worry.

What will the pain be like? Are implants the right choice? What will recovery look like? Will I be at all comfortable in my new body?

I don't want to be around anyone this morning. I know my parents are likely very anxious and I cannot allow that energy to move to me. I decide to calm myself with meditation and stretching. There is comfort in being alone. In the solitude. In the quiet.

As I stand in the shower, doing my presurgical wash, I sob. For so long I have spoken negatively about my boobs, and here I am, about to lose them. I take extra time washing them. I close my eyes. No longer able to tell the difference between the shower water and the tears, as both stream down my body, I allow myself to think about this tremendous loss. This last shower will be forever burned in my mind.

While the unknowns induce natural worry, I also feel incredibly confident. My best friend Layton texts me to let me know she is thinking of me, and my response is one of confidence:

"I got this and I know it! I can feel myself surrounded by so much love! It's like nothing I've ever felt before, Layton! It's G-d or spirit or whatever we choose to call it! It's there and I am witnessing it!"

The first stop this morning is Dr. Mann's office to "get marked up."

All I can think about are the old movies and TV shows showing women having their fat circled as part of pledging a sorority. A beautiful college girl is in some sort of "hell week" when the older sisters bring her down to the sorority house in the middle of the night, tell her to undress, and then use a Sharpie to circle the fatty areas of her body.

I can't think of too many more humiliating things.

Just for the record, I am in a sorority and this never once happened. It's totally a made-up legend.

Nevertheless, I still have this image in my mind and am certain it is what I will experience. All I can picture in my head is Dr. Mann taking a thick black marker to my skin and circling the areas for surgery.

I stand here now, in yet another medical gown, in front of Dr. Mann, just hours before my breasts will be removed. My stomach flips. I start to sweat. It all feels too real now.

"We need to mark up the areas for surgery. Even though I won't be doing any surgery until after Dr. Bender performs your bilateral mastectomy and removes any lymph nodes, I need to do this now, while you're standing, so the marks are accurately reflected in this upright position."

I slowly remove my gown and he has some back and forth with the assistant in the room with us. He stands in front of me, makes evaluations, and begins to measure areas and make marks on my chest. While this is for surgical purposes, and he isn't circling fat, I still feel intensely exposed and vulnerable.

After he leaves the room, I tell Derek to take a picture of my body. I shock myself with the words as they exit my mouth, but I want to be able to look back on this moment and possibly see the bravery I can't notice in myself right now.

I get dressed, yet despite having clothes on, I've never felt more naked.

I have no time to think about this, though, as we need to get to the hospital on time, and we are now cutting it close. With robotic movements, I walk out the door and push away the reality of what is about to happen.

Derek and I drive down the street to the hospital and check in. We wait about ten minutes before I am called back to presurgery. Once I am set up here, Derek will be able to come back and be with me until I am taken into surgery. The surgery is expected to take several hours.

As I walk back with the nurse, I notice my nerves begin to feel more unsettled. I realize that while I have been confident this morning, a part of me has likely been trying to convince me that if I am prepared, speak positively, and enter enough uplifting mantras in my journal, then all is fine. Once in the "room," I change into the surgical gown, socks, and hairnet. I notice my breathing has deepened. I am indeed nervous. Of course I am! I am about to have major surgery and lose my fucking breasts. A sterile chill is in the air. The nurses cover me with warm blankets but, no matter how many they layer on, it doesn't seem to help. I am chilled to the bone.

Over the course of the next thirty minutes or so, several different nurses enter my room. They all wear scrubs, clogs, name tags and they all ask the same questions, "Can you please state your full name and birth date?" "Are you allergic to any medications?" and, "When was the last time you had something to eat or drink?" My favorite is when they ask me, "What procedure are you having today and who is the surgeon?" While I understand this is their protocol, the repetition increases my anxiety. With each answer I can hear the irritability and impatience in my voice increase.

Derek returns, which signals to me that pre-check is complete. Rather than cry or share my fears, I point to a sign that hangs on the white wall behind my hospital bed. It says "No Photos Allowed." I then show him the few pictures I've already taken of myself while nurses weren't in the room. I'm smiling and giving a thumbs up to the camera. We press our luck with the rule and take a silly selfie with the "No Cameras" sign behind us. Even in this dark moment, rather than allow myself to feel afraid, I put up my armor and smile.

All will be fine.

All is fine.

IV in. Consents signed. Premedications given.

It is time.

Derek leans down and gives me two kisses, our signature kiss. As I am wheeled down the hallway, I stare at my breasts and thank them for being a beautiful part of me and for nourishing my babies.

We're in the operating room and my anxiety peaks again.

What if the anesthesia doesn't work? What if I feel something? I hate the oxygen mask they'll put on. I don't want this.

Tears begin to well up. People move all around the room. They talk to me but I don't process. It feels like I'm on a TV show, watching myself from the outside. Someone moves closer to me and I can tell she's about to place an oxygen mask over my mouth and nose.

"Wait. I am really claustrophobic and anxious. Will you be giving me meds soon to help me calm down? I need it."

"Oh yes, honey. You'll be getting a nice cocktail soon and you'll be heading to sleep."

The next thing I know I'm being wheeled around on the hospital bed.

The room is spinning. My stomach tightens and flips. I notice I'm holding a hospital vomit bag.

How did that get there?

I hear Derek's voice but am too foggy to speak back. I hear the wheels of the bed against the hospital tiles. I smell something familiar, like gum or a candy cane.

What is that?

I manage to tell Derek I'm going to throw up. He brings the bag closer to my mouth and I notice he moves something on my shoulder.

Peppermint. It's peppermint.

He has moved the peppermint-soaked cotton balls resting on my shoulder a bit closer to my face.

Wow. Leigh would be so happy to know they're using essential oils in the hospital.

Once in my recovery room, things begin to become a little clearer around me. I can see and hear the nurses. They tell Derek things went well and I'll be in this recovery room for about an hour before they transfer me to my own room. A bilateral mastectomy is actually considered outpatient surgery but my doctors want me to be monitored overnight since I once had a postsurgical blood clot.

As I continue to become more awake in recovery, the nausea is still very present and the pain begins to increase. I hate when doctors ask me to rate my pain on a scale of one to ten, as if everyone's one to ten is the same. In this particular moment, nobody needs to ask. It is clear my pain is way above a ten. With pain meds administered through the IV, I trade pain for the side effects of insane headache, nausea, and fogginess.

Visiting hours end, and it is time for Derek to head home for the night. I cry with fear. I don't want to be alone. Yes, the medical staff is here, but I don't want to be by myself for even a minute. We ask if he's allowed to sleep in the room but, alas, the answer is no. No matter where my relationship stands with him at any point in time, we are always there for each other. He is somewhat of a security blanket in life and now I have to let him go. All while in pain and feeling awful. We exchange two light kisses on the lips. "I'll be back in the morning," and then he is gone.

Soon after I am wheeled from recovery to my private room and slowly, cautiously settled into my new bed by the nurses. Over the course of the next several hours, life becomes much like it did after having a baby. It is all routine for the staff. Instead of changing diapers, feeding the baby, and watching him sleep, they are changing the pad I lie on, as the fluid from the surgical drains have soiled it, emptying the drains, measuring the fluid in the drains, administering pain meds, checking vitals, checking my incisions, and emptying my catheter. In between rotations I dose off, either out of exhaustion or from the meds.

Surgical drains are something I've never experienced before. I have two drains, one coming out from each side of my chest, just next to my breasts. Each has a tube that was inserted into my skin during surgery. The tube collects fluid from my body and drains it into a bulb at the other end of each tube. Dr. Mann told me about the drains and his nurse had reviewed instructions for draining, so we'll be prepared once at home. I'll measure and spill out this fluid often until my body produces a low enough amount that the drains can then be removed. It seems like a simple process, except I am very squeamish. Even a loose tooth being wiggled gives me the heebie-jeebies. Draining my own fluid sounds next level.

Time creeps by in the hospital. Hours feel like days, despite the cycling routine and my short winks of sleep.

It takes everything in my body to move to ring the call button.

"My pain is unbearable. It's excruciating. It's as if the meds just aren't working anymore," I say into the air, as if speaking to G-d. The nurse on the receiving end is somewhat of a savior after all.

I chuckle inside, as I think about how I brought my journal, as if I'd actually journal here while I recover.

Oh, sweet Amy. You had no idea this would be so hard.

POST-SURGERY

Bricks on my chest. Throbbing. Stabbing down into my arms. Everything hurts. Every movement feels like torture. I've delivered three babies vaginally and have never felt pain like this.

I think back to when I initially held the tissue expander in Dr. Mann's office and realize I was correct about it hurting once placed inside of me.

It hurts to move at all. Yet movement is necessary.

Desperately trying to shift myself in the uncomfortable hospital bed in an attempt to bring some comfort. With catheter removed, using the bathroom now requires assisted walking from a nurse. Turning on my side to sit up and get out of the bed. Every second causing lightning bolts through my body. Gingerly raising my left hand and arm just enough to ring the nurses call button.

Each of these movements is a game of *"How badly do I really need to?"*

I need to pee. I can't hold it in any longer. I endure the pain it takes to call the nurse's station, tell them what I need, and have them help me out of bed.

There is a certain vulnerability in speaking into the call button, "I need to go to the bathroom," and having someone assist you in the process. I know they are nurses and I am not too shy about anything, yet there's a level of intrusion and discomfort. I've gotten over it pretty quickly and much of the time the nurses step out, leaving the bathroom door open to provide me some privacy.

I stand up from the bed and immediately feel dizzy. I relay this to the nurse who is holding me up and steadying me. Her long brown curls hang from her head down into my space.

"Take it slow. Sit back down."

I try again. One hand holds the IV pole, the nurse holds the other hand. I make it the few steps to the bathroom.

"I'm really dizzy. I think I'm going to throw up."

She guides me a few more steps to sit on the toilet. My head is lowered and all I see are her shoes and the tile floor. I'm sweating profusely. Everything is spinning.

In a ninja-like move, she quickly reaches behind her for a vomit bag.

"Keep your head up and breathe Amy," I hear her say.

Words frantically come out of my mouth: "I'm going to pass out. I can feel it. I'm going to pass out. This happened once before after another surgery."

My head lowers and eyes close. Everything goes black.

Cold cloths on my head. Ice packs maybe.
Voices. Nurses talking.
I'm completely out of breath.
Did I pee yet?
What just happened?

I hear, "Amy. Amy. Take deep breaths. You passed out. It's okay. You're okay. We need you to breathe."

I try to deepen my breath. I try to talk, but it is a challenge. Slowly, I begin to feel awake. It feels like we've been in this bathroom much longer than we have. In reality, it's only been a few minutes. I fully come to and I'm scared.

What just happened?
Was it a vasovagal response like I had after my knee surgery all those years ago?
Is it a blood clot?

After I'm steadied, I explain I've had this happen before and was told it's a vasovagal response, where my body overreacts to emotional stress, causing my heart rate and blood pressure to drop suddenly and making me faint. She agrees it's most likely this and has already paged the doctor on call to evaluate me as well. With the nurse's help, I steady myself enough to move my gown aside, pull down the lovely mesh hospital underwear, and pee. This time the nurse does not leave my side. I am quite unnerved and appreciate the extra caution she takes.

All this because I had to pee and managed to press that damn call button.

Later the doctor is evaluating me and decides I'll stay another night to be monitored and ensure I don't have another episode. I'm reassured by this, especially since my pain level is still incredibly high, although it has become more bearable. I'm not sure if that's because the meds are working better and the pain is decreasing or if it's because I'm simply tolerating it. On that dumb scale, I'd say it's moved down to a nine or ten, rather than in the teens or higher.

Derek arrives and I try to fill him in on what happened but I'm too tired. He tells me to rest and as I dose off the nurse comes in to complete her routine of vitals, drains, and meds. Again. Everything looks good I'm told. She recounts the events for Derek so he is caught up.

"Never a dull moment with you, babe," he says with a wink.

Derek stays with me most of the day while my parents take care of the boys at home. I sound like a broken record as I cry and tell him how bad the pain is. My tears are filled with frustration and anger. I sleep on and off for most of the day with multiple checks from nurses and doctors disrupting this rest. It's maddening at times. I just want to sleep. I don't want to feel this pain. Instead, it's changing the bed pad, emptying, measuring, and recording the drain fluid, administering a cocktail of pain meds, and checking vitals and my incisions. Derek advocates for me and continues to tell them I'm maybe only down to a nine in pain. The surgeon on rounds tells us this is normal and it will continue to get better over time.

This is normal? I want to be in my own bed, but I'm scared to leave the care of the nurses.

Night number two is fairly uneventful. Just the rotation of ringing the call bell to pee, nurses coming in to change the bed pad, empty, measure, and record the drain fluid, administer my cocktail of pain meds, and, of course, check my vitals and my incisions.

Derek and I take a few pictures, and we are smiling. Perhaps it's a good moment? Perhaps I am covering up some of the pain?

It's morning, day three, and I'm downright grateful and elated about being able to stomach a cup of coffee (albeit hospital coffee), some scrambled eggs, and fruit. My entire chest is still throbbing, but at least I have an appetite. The pain meds have been making me so incredibly nauseated.

The nurses spend time with Derek and me reviewing how to properly milk (squeeze) the drains and collect and record the fluid color and amount. At this point I'm over the ick factor this gave me a few days ago, but Derek doesn't look as at ease. This is the man who almost passed out during the labor and delivery of Jacob, our second child. He blames it on a lack of eating but I've never let him live it down.

Derek gathers my belongings and pulls the car around front. I'm being disconnected from IVs and steadily moved into a wheelchair by the nurse. I stare at the tile floor. I'm scared and ready to be home at the same time.

"You did really great, Amy," the nurse says as she begins wheeling me down the hall.

"Thanks. This is definitely harder and more painful than I expected. I hope the pain gets better soon."

"You're starting to respond to the medications orally, which is a good sign. You have a wonderfully supportive husband. I think you're going to be just fine. I'm wishing you all the best."

"Thank you," I say with a smile, even though she can't see it through my face mask. *There's COVID for you, again!*

She wheels me right up to the car and Derek helps me get in the passenger seat. He gingerly places little pillows on my breasts and gently fastens the seatbelt. I hold the pillows in place, in the hopes they will ease the discomfort of this ride.

We get home and I feel overwhelmed as soon as I approach the door.

How am I going to do this without the nurses? How am I going to take care of myself and *be a mom? When will I be able to work again? Why am I still in so much pain?*

My boys hesitantly hug me, very gently, and tell me, "I love you." They are just the sweetest. I hate they have to see me like this. It's certainly not the picture I had of myself as a mother, at any point in time.

"These were the longest couple of days," my mom says as she embraces me in a hug I think we both need. It's a hug, but not a real hug. She can't squeeze me. My mom is known for her good hugs and, until this moment, I never realized just how much I love and need them.

A sadness washes over me and I back away. My body is anxious and wriggly. It's all too much. I know from therapy I can't allow her emotions to become my own and it's so challenging. She is my mother, and rightfully so, her fear is palpable. Her compassion comes across as pity. I know she doesn't mean it, though. She only wants to help and wishes I didn't have to go through this.

My dad looks at me with a mixture of love, care, and shock. His arms wrap around me and he lowers his lips to my forehead, delivering his signature forehead kisses. I don't think he was prepared for all this. I can't blame him. None of us were prepared for any of this shit. We separate and smile at each other.

"I didn't know you'd have those drains coming out of your body, Amy. It kills me to see you going through this, honey."

I'm incredibly grateful for the relationship I have with my parents. I know they will always be by my side through anything, and I appreciate them being here now.

The next week is an absolute clusterfuck. The pain becomes unbearable. Stabbing, throbbing pain. My sister comes over and we attempt to watch a light rom-com, but within minutes my eyes are closing. Not only are the meds not helping but they're also making me feel dizzy, tired, and light-headed.

My days are a cycle of caring for myself. In between changing suture dressings, crying, and measuring the burnt-sienna-colored fluid from the drains, I attempt to take a few steps outside every day. Most times I walk these gentle, slow steps with my mom and dad on each side of me. I feel so cared for, so loved, and so lucky. Yet I remain filled with frustration at the slow process of healing.

A light breaks through the darkness when one of my best friends, Courtney, flies up from Savannah, Georgia. She has come all this way to spend the day—yes, the day—with me. I am incredibly blessed to have many supportive and loving friends, and Courtney is definitely one of them! We met several years ago, and what started out as a business relationship quickly developed into a deep friendship. She always shows up for me, offering words of encouragement, a boost of confidence when I need it, and a glass of bubbly to toast our friendship when we're together. There won't be any bubbly today, just Court sitting by my side as I rest and recover.

She pauses the movie we're watching, looks over at me, and says, "I have to tell you. I was, of course, feeling for you after the surgery, but being here with you, it all really hits me. Seeing you with the breast pillows; seeing all your medications lined up and the chart for when you take each one. I'm so glad I can be here for you and I'm also glad I'm able to better understand and feel what you are going through. It's really hard to do that from so far away."

We don't get to see each other often, which makes this day even more special. The day goes too fast and, unfortunately, it is time for her to fly back home. We exchange long hugs and shed tears as she gets in her rental car to head to the airport. To have a friend like Courtney is to have a treasured gift in life. One day together is never enough for us.

The next day is my group therapy, and I somehow muster up the physical and emotional energy to log on virtually. I feel the need for some normalcy and this seems to be it. Everyone seems so happy to see me. At first, I think I'll need to slip back into my happy, positive role, and I really don't want to.

Be real, Amy. That's what you're here for.

"How are you doing, Amy?" Martha asks.

"You look kinda pale," adds Tom.

I'm so tired and can barely keep my eyes open. I want to smile and say, "I'm fine," but thankfully the truth spills out of me like a schoolgirl sharing the latest gossip.

"I fucking hate this. I'm in so much pain and the meds aren't really working. They told me being at a nine pain level is normal. That doesn't seem normal to me. What did I do to deserve this? I'm so tired, mentally and physically. Between the drains and the rotation of meds, it's like a full-time job. I'm totally flooded. I don't know what to do."

I grab a tissue to wipe the tears from my face and blow my nose. I'm a total mess. I breathe deeply to calm myself, manage my signature smile, and I apologize for my rant. Of course I apologize, the "nice girl, people pleaser" I am. I'm called out for this.

They're mad for me. Some say it out loud and with others I can just feel it. They seem most angered by the way Derek and I have been shirked off by the doctors each time we've told them about my pain levels. Their outrage brings me comfort and relief around sharing my authentic feelings in this moment.

"Amy, you need to be resting and recovering. Derek needs to step in and step up here. He needs to call the plastic surgeon, the breast surgeon, and whoever else needs to be called until he gets a resolution as to how they can treat this pain. This is unacceptable. He needs to advocate for you and get this taken care of," Martha strongly asserts.

I know she's right and I nod in agreement. They know me well enough to know I'd likely take this on myself and make the calls, so they make me promise I will have Derek do it. I promise and we continue with the remainder of the therapy session. I'm there, but I'm not. The pain has gotten so bad, I know I need another pill, but I don't want to take it. I don't want to feel the side effects. I let them know that I have to go and log off the meeting.

I warily raise myself out of the recliner that has become my home and make my way to the bathroom for my pain pills and essential oils. I sigh as I see myself in the mirror. I'm overcome by a sinking feeling in my stomach.

Stop it, Amy. Yes, you're in pain. It's not the worst thing ever. Go for a walk. Move your body and change a feeling, right? That's what you always say.

With my emotions shoved down, I carefully take the steps downstairs and outside. I'm so frustrated by how slow I have to walk and the pain I endure with each step.

I ask my mom to go for a little walk with me before the meds kick in.

Is she wondering whether the surgery was enough or if there will be more? She has to bathe me, dress me, and hold me, all things she did when I was a child. Is she afraid? No mother should go through this with their child at any age.

Deliveries of food, flowers, cards, and gifts keep my spirits up as we wait for pathology reports. The strong community I've built throughout my life is showing up in big ways.

I see neighborhood acquaintances on my walks. They ask how I'm doing and I'm unsure how to answer. Do I say I'm fine to keep them comfortable and keep the conversation short, or should I be honest with them and allow them to feel bad for me, ask me how they can help, and look at me with pity and fear? They tell me how great I look. How strong I am. I hear lots of, "You've got this!" and, "You're such a warrior!" and, "I'm praying for you!" These sentiments fall flat and leave me frustrated. I know everyone is being kind, and it's all the same things I've said to others before being in this situation myself. Now I want to shout back, "I feel like shit! I look like shit! I don't want to be strong or a warrior. I'm just doing what you would do. I'm doing what I have to do to survive!"

But I keep all this to myself and usually give a smile, tell them, "Each day is different," and thank them for their prayers.

Derek has spoken to Dr. Mann and a new cocktail of meds is prescribed.

As I recover, I maintain my belief that, with my breasts taken, the cancer is out of my body and this will be it.

The pathology will yield clean results. No radiation. No chemo. No further treatment. Just checkups and returning to some sense of normalcy, whatever that may look like.

PATHOLOGY
(2/25/21–2/26/21)

It has been nine days since my surgery. The pain is still intolerable. I rock methodically in the glider in our living room. My parents sit on the couch and watch TV. I notice I've missed a call from the breast surgeon's office and she has left a voicemail. I told Derek earlier that, if it happens, I won't be able to handle the pathology coming back with bad news and me needing treatment. Surgery, fine. Treatment, nope. I'm at my limit. I won't even say the word "chemo" out loud, fearful of making it a reality.

I hit play, listen to the message, and begin sobbing.

"No, no, no," I repeat.

"What, what is it?" my mom and dad both ask.

I tap the play button again, tap speaker, and Dr. Bender's voice fills the room. I am in agony all over again.

"Hi, Amy. This is Dr. Bender. I just wanted to call and talk with you about the pathology that's come back. We will talk in-depth about it tomorrow, but I don't want to slow things down. I want Jane [her coordinator] to go ahead and start to make some other appointments for you, so don't be freaked out when you see other appointments [in your online patient portal]. I'm going to have you meet with the radiation oncologist and with the medical oncologist because, as I think you know, I was pretty concerned there'd be some invasive cancer found and there was. You can call me back at the office today. I just want Jane to be able to start to move on making appointments for you. My cell is... and I can give you an overview of things and then tomorrow we can go over everything in detail. I hope you're recovering well and I will talk to you soon. Okay, bye-bye."

I can barely breathe. It's as if I'm stuck underwater, holding my breath for dear life. Tears seem inevitable and then flood out.

Don't be freaked out? Of course I'm freaking out! And I'm in so much pain. I can't make it through much more.

My mom comes over to hug me and I can feel the heat of fear as it radiates throughout her body. My dad starts to play the message again.

This cannot be about them, Amy. Do what you need to do for you!

I back out of my mom's embrace and I bark, "Take it outside, Dad, please! I can't listen to it again!"

I look at my mom as she sits across from me on the little footrest that accompanies the glider. I feel like a little girl who needs her mom. I need to be comforted. I want to be heard and given space for my emotions.

"I can't do this mom. I don't think I can take any more."

"You will, Amy. You'll do whatever it takes. You'll do it for those boys," she says behind tears of her own.

"And I'll do it for me, Mom."

Why can't anything ever simply be about me? For me?

This brief exchange immediately transports me back in time to a conversation I'd had with my mom a few years ago when Derek and I were struggling in our marriage. She had said something along the lines of, "Amy, you have three young kids to think about," to which I'd replied, "You think I don't know that. I also have myself to think about, Mom." At that time, what she viewed as selfish I saw as self-preservation.

Of course I know I'll do whatever I need to stay alive and kill this cancer, but right now it just doesn't seem fair. It's unfathomable. First, a cancer diagnosis. Then a bilateral mastectomy. And now, invasive cancer.

I'm mad that the breast surgeon made it seem so unlikely that there would be anything invasive, and now her message makes it seem like she had believed otherwise all along. It feels like a deep betrayal.

Why didn't anyone prepare me better for this possibility?

It is not lost on me that I receive this news as I sit in the glider where I breastfed each of my children and rocked them to sleep over many years. I rub my hand along the textured fabric of the armrest as my thoughts wander down a rabbit hole.

My boys. My precious boys. How will I tell them? Will they understand? How much more can they take?

Derek comes home from an appointment about twenty minutes later. I'm still sitting in the glider. I haven't been able to move since listening to the message. I'm in shock. I appear obviously distraught and tell him we need to go upstairs. As soon as we get into our bedroom, I break down and cry again.

"What is it, Amy? Oh g-d, what is it?" he pleads.

Between my sobs, I manage to say the words I dread having to say. "I got a message from Dr. B. The cancer is invasive."

In an instant, his arms are wrapped around me in a hug. I play the voicemail message for him. As he listens, he glances up at me, and we both shake our heads in astonishment and pure disbelief. Even after listening to it multiple times now, I'm in denial.

This can't be happening! It's a bad dream, Amy. Wake up.

It definitely is not my imagination. It is very real and I cannot comprehend it at all. I want and need to know more, to understand what this means for me. My hands shake as I return Dr. Bender's call.

She restates what she said in the voicemail. She's so matter-of-fact. I feel dismissed. I can't make sense of how this change in diagnosis and treatment doesn't seem to upend her as much as it does me.

Had she actually thought this was more of a possibility than I thought she conveyed? Is this just so routine for her that she can't be emotional about it?

"We'll go over this in more detail at your appointment tomorrow. I'll be sure you understand and feel confident about the next steps."

The rest of the day and night are a complete blur. Between the pain, the medications, and this news, my mind, body, and spirit are all numb.

The next morning I wake from my short slumber, and for a moment I think maybe it was all just a bad dream. My eyes sting from crying, pain arises where my breasts once were, and my stomach turns—all reminders this is most definitely real. I can't get out of bed. Exhaustion and the mere thought of what lies ahead make me cry with anger and fear.

Derek gets the boys up and ready for school, and I just lie there as I wait for my mom to come and help me get ready. Only ten days post-surgery, I still require help with my most basic needs, in this case bathing and cleaning out my surgical drains and dressing. I don't know how much time has passed when my mom walks into my bedroom. She sits down on the bed beside me and we exchange a look. Her eyes say, "I'm so sorry, my sweet girl. I love you so much," and mine say,

"This shouldn't be happening, Mom. I love you." I know if we sit here any longer, I will break down, so I slowly begin to sit up, and she helps me the rest of the way. I wince in pain.

"What is it, Amy? Are you okay?"

"I'm in so much pain, Mom. But I need to get ready to go. I just need to move slowly."

I walk to the bathroom at a snail's pace. My chest pounds more with every step. I need to take my pain meds again, but that requires eating, which I have no desire to do. I have zero energy to shower, but know being a bit cleaner will help me feel even a little better. My mom helps me undress. I feel weak. I sit down on the side of the bathtub and take a few deep breaths. I need to empty the surgical drains into their little medicine measuring cups and record the amount and color of the fluid collected. She helps me as I begin the process of unhooking the drains from my surgical bra and moving them to the lanyards hanging from my neck like necklaces. I'm completely wiped out before I make it into the shower. Tears of defeat fall. I simply can't stop them. We don't even acknowledge them. At this point tears are pretty much a constant and we know what they mean.

Sadness. Fear. Exhaustion. Anger.

Is this my new normal?

I steadily make my way the few steps from the bathtub to the shower and sit down on the medical shower stool. I feel absolutely helpless as my mom bathes me and washes my hair, so cautiously and carefully. I begin to imagine what this is like for her and how she's feeling. A mother bathing her forty-three-year-old daughter, washing the scars covering her chest, knowing this is now only the beginning of a long healing process.

It is once again time to carry my little green notebook to another doctor's appointment. It contains a list of questions I have for Dr. B.

What stage is my cancer?
Will you need to take more lymph nodes?
Will I have any other type of imaging done to rule out cancer elsewhere in my body?
What's the ruling with COVID and having visitors?
Can I get my COVID vaccine?
If the cancer was found in lymph nodes that have been removed, why do I need treatment?
How will this impact my exchange surgery timeline?

We sit in the same waiting room as last time but it feels much different now. Rather than look at the other women there, I focus on myself and how I might appear to them. Between my mastectomy shirt and the drains that hang a little too low to remain hidden, it is obvious I've just had surgery. I can't worry about that, though. I have bigger concerns on my mind.

As we sit and listen to Dr. B share how both of the lymph nodes taken have come back from pathology as positive with cancer, I begin to feel dizzy. A hot sensation travels down my body. My stomach is queasy.

I'm going to pass out. It's happening again.

I slowly sip my water with hopes it will help.

"I don't feel well. I need air. I feel like I'm going to pass out. Like I did in the hospital after surgery," I interrupt.

"I know. It's a lot of information..." she continues, but I no longer hear her words.

Derek leaps into action, asks whether they have crackers, juice, or anything. No, they do not. Dr. B places a cool, wet paper towel around my neck and another on my forehead. Derek decides to drive down the street to CVS and get something for me to eat.

Dr. B walks out to check on another patient while we wait for Derek. A nurse comes in to be with me.

Moments later Dr. B returns with a few dark chocolates.

"These are from my secret stash."

I smile and graciously accept them. I peel open the foil wrapper and take a small bite. The creamy, cocoa flavor fills my mouth. I suck on it, afraid that if I swallow and take another bite I'll eat them too fast. I need these three little chocolates to last until Derek returns with food.

I notice the nurse has left and I'm alone. Fear washes over me.

Seriously? They left me here alone? I'm so dizzy. Maybe I should lie down? No, that might make it worse. Why would they leave me alone in here right now?

The cool paper towels have begun to fall apart, but I continue to press them on my head and neck while I slowly savor each small bite of dark chocolate, allowing it to melt in my mouth.

Derek returns with a six-pack of applesauce cups and a box of spoons. His face is panic-stricken when he sees I've been left alone. We exchange a look, which silently says, "What the fuck?" but we are both too distraught to speak actual words.

Dr. Bender returns, and as I sit on the exam table slowly spooning applesauce into my mouth, she starts to run through a litany of information. I catch only pieces.

"Stage 2B, grade 3."

"Oncologist."

"Chemotherapy."

"HER2-positive"

"Radiation oncologist."

"Targeted radiation."

"Jane is checking your insurance and scheduling appointments for you."

"You're going to be okay. We've still caught this early."

Okay? I'm going to be okay? I'm not okay right now!"

Dr. B reassures me these doctors are the best of the best and I will be in good hands with them. I ask questions written in my little green notebook. Questions based on things I've read online. Questions from my parents and my sister.

She says most of the questions are ones to ask the oncologist and the radiation oncologist.

I nod as she speaks. I'm numb again.

How did we get here? How are these the questions I have to navigate?

I'm like a child following the leader at school as we walk with her down the hallway to Jane's office. I didn't think I'd be in this office again.

All the cancer was supposed to be taken away with my breasts. I'm going to be okay, though. I said I'd embrace cancer and that is what I'll do. I need to be the strong one in all this.

Meanwhile, terror and agitation bubble over inside my body.

Derek sits next to me, and once again I wonder what's running through his mind in this moment. Jane is just as tender and compassionate as the first time we found ourselves in her office. It must be hard to be the one walking people through this part of the process.

"You are an angel and I really appreciate you," are the only words I get out as she's sharing the information contained on a sheet of paper outlining my upcoming appointments.

When she reaches the end of the schedule, she acknowledges the overwhelm and asks me how I'm doing.

I'm misty-eyed and the tears come again as soon as I open my mouth.

"I'm really scared. I never expected this. It was supposed to just be surgery."

She validates my feelings and suggests I schedule an appointment with the psychiatrist available through Living with Cancer services. She shares his name and number and I add it to my little green notebook. I'm beginning to hate this little green notebook.

JOURNAL ENTRY (2/26/21)

―

I know I can do this and will conquer, but it doesn't take away from the fact I don't want to do this. I have done hard things, but they've been my choice to conquer. And I feel I trained for many. Not this. I'm just so mad! I've worked so hard to take care of my body, my mind, and my health. It just doesn't make any sense. How the fuck do I have cancer? Before surgery I said I could handle whatever came my way from it, but if I had to endure treatment I'd lose my fucking mind. Now here I am. How am I going to do this? Why have I been given this to conquer?

All I can do is cry, even though it hurts physically. I need to know I'm going to be able to manage this, mentally, emotionally, and physically.

How will I be a mom? The way I want to be a mom. How will Derek and I get through this? How will I work? And him? Who will take the best care of me? Why the fuck are we being given this?

I know I can do it. I can do hard things, but I don't want to!

I'll feel better once we have and know the plan too.

OFFICE OF ONCOLOGY (3/1/21)

We approach Dr. Ramirez's office and the sign saying "Oncology." I find it completely inconceivable that we are here. I've tried to reconcile my thoughts and reality over the past few days, and it's been a struggle.

All that has occurred in the past two months—which feels like two years—has me questioning so much of what I've believed and taught for years.

Can one even be a "serial optimist"? Can we find ways to move away from fear in times when it feels all-consuming? Are we really manifesting our future? Because, if so, why the fuck do I have cancer?

I ring the bell as indicated and a woman comes to the door to do a verbal COVID screening before we can enter. Ironically, I'm wearing a mask with a big smile on it. She compliments my mask and I say thank you in a high-pitched voice. If one didn't know any better, they would think I was having a great day. I sound upbeat and delighted, like I'm thanking my server at my favorite restaurant as opposed to heading into my first appointment with a medical oncologist.

I check in at the front desk. My hand shakes as I fill out the required paperwork. My feelings inside indeed do not match those I'm portraying on the outside.

As we sit in the waiting room, I glance down at Derek's lap, which holds the "Bible of Breast Cancer" we received from Dr. Bender. I look over the questions I've noted in my handy little green notebook. Tears begin to form in the corners of my eyes and I blink them away.

After being called back to the exam room, changing into yet another gown—this one is pink of all colors! I don't want anything pink! Pink equals breast cancer and I've had enough with this shit!—repeating my name, birthday, meds, and allergies yet again, and having my vitals taken, we wait for Dr. Ramirez. It doesn't take long before she greets us.

She's a petite woman, who looks to be somewhat older than me, but her beautiful blonde hair and stylish choice in shoes could indicate otherwise. She wins me over right way when she asks how I am doing and how my recovery from surgery has been. Much like Dr. Bender, she seems straightforward and clinical with a side of warmheartedness.

My pen begins to pick up speed as I take notes on her medical jargon. Words and acronyms I have no idea are about to become a part of my general vernacular.

"Your cancer is estrogen/progesterone negative and HER2-positive, so you'll be receiving TCHP chemo. These letters represent each of the medicines: Taxotere, Carboplatin, Herceptin, and Perjeta. You'll come in every three weeks, for six rounds. After that you will have completed the TC portion and will finish out the HP, receiving it every three weeks for the remainder of a full year from day one."

A year? I'm going to be doing this for a year? That seems like a really long time. Am I going to feel sick all that time?

I move around in my chair as she continues, "The one major concern with Herceptin is that it can cause heart muscle damage and heart failure. Because of this, you'll need to have echocardiograms every four months and see a cardio-oncologist throughout the year."

Heart failure? That sounds serious. Why am I taking this drug?

I share my concern with Dr. Ramirez and she reassures me that, in her opinion, these risks are unlikely and worth taking in order to kill any residual cancer and prevent metastasis. When she is finished, I ask Derek for the "Breast Cancer Bible" and ask her a few questions that are recommended to ask your medical oncologist. It's the only page I've referenced in the entire book.

"Should I eat before treatments?"

"A light meal is recommended. You'll be taking a steroid beforehand and you'll want to eat with that."

"Can I continue taking vitamins and supplements?"

"No. We don't know the exact interactions of different supplements and vitamins with TCHP, so we recommend you stop taking all these."

She takes a step back and casually leans against the wall. Perhaps she's settling in for what she thinks may be many more questions.

"After I complete treatment, how often will I return for checkups?"

"We will create a schedule then, but usually it starts off monthly, then every other month, every six months, and eventually annually."

"How will you evaluate the effectiveness of the treatments?"

"We will be looking for a positive response to the chemo when you have your exchange surgery and Dr. Bender takes lymph nodes."

"Will I continue to get my period?"

"Your periods will most likely stop during treatment. Based on your age there is really a fifty-fifty chance as to whether they will return after that time."

I lean back in the chair, sigh, and let her know that's all I've got for now. I'm sure I'll have more later.

She has already answered the remaining listed questions throughout our time together. Even if she hadn't, my brain can't take any more information. Derek and I have both been taking notes. I'm certain my parents will have more questions.

A change in her body language indicates she is moving to the next thing.

She explains that, based on the pathology reports, she wants to start chemo as quickly as possible. This would ensure the highest rate of success. Before leaving the office, Dr. Ramirez gives us a tour of the infusion suite where my treatments will take place.

Inside the infusion suite are seven rooms or bays, each separated by a wall and enclosed by a curtain. I note small artwork hanging throughout, nurses filled with positivity and smiles, and hospital-style overhead lighting. I make eye contact with a couple of the women in their bay and give a smirk of solidarity. One has lost her hair and I wonder when that will be me.

My first chemo treatment is scheduled for March 17—St. Patrick's Day and my niece's birthday. Perhaps that will bring good luck.

I have quite a few boxes to check before then.

ALL THE CHEMO PREP

Before I can start checking the pre-chemo boxes, I have a follow-up appointment scheduled with my plastic surgeon, Dr. Mann. As planned, he fills my tissue expanders with saline. With a look of sadness for me, he tells me that while he hoped I'd be back for future fills, he can't do any once I start chemo. I will have to hope the tissue expands enough for the implants I'll receive after chemo. As in our past encounters, he makes me feel like an individual, not just a patient, as he genuinely wishes me the best of luck with chemo and says he will see me at future checkups.

I also have an introductory appointment with Dr. Conner, a radiation oncologist. Dr. Ramirez and Dr. Bender have assured me he's the best of the best. He's the head of the department, so I feel I'm in good hands. After this long appointment I'm glad Derek was there with me to help remember all the information. We will see Dr. Conner again after chemo and my exchange to implants surgery.

The first pre-chemo box to check is making sure I am negative for COVID, so I head to get tested. I also need to have some blood work completed as well as my initial echocardiogram to record baseline reports.

I spoke with Dr. Ramirez about the chronic pain I've dealt with for years, which has been ruled autoimmune, and how my fear now is that it's cancer all over my body. I know this isn't likely, but at this point nothing seems impossible. She agreed it's likely not related but ordered a bone scan to confirm it is indeed not cancer.

All these appointments and tests are squeezed in between March 13 and 15. It's busy and chaotic, which is probably for the best, so I don't have to focus on what it's all for—chemotherapy.

Next up, Derek and I head to a "Teaching Appointment" with the nurse practitioner, Melissa, at Dr. Ramirez's office. We sit around a small table and she begins to go over information that seems so rote for her. I get it; this is stuff she's likely explained hundreds of times. But for us it is all new. It is like a foreign language we cannot comprehend.

She starts at the beginning, explaining that for two days leading up to chemo I'll need to take a steroid, Decadron, at home. I take a deep breath and immediately pipe up, "I've had to take a steroid before and it gave me awful headaches."

We're off to a great start here!

"It's really important you take the steroid to minimize the side effects and allergic reactions during treatment. I think you should try it and see how it goes. Does that sound okay to you?"

I nod in agreement and she moves to the next item on her list.

"On the day of treatment, before we administer any chemo drugs, you will receive several premeds. These include an additional dose of the steroid, Benadryl to also prevent any allergic reactions, Tylenol for pain, and antinausea meds. Some will be taken orally and some through IV."

Holy crap! That's a lot of things going into my body, and we haven't even gotten to the chemo part yet.

Perhaps she sees the overwhelm in my eyes, as she adds, "The nurses will be right near you and will make sure you are doing okay."

Her finger moves down her list as she begins talking about chemo.

"You'll be having a mediport placed. Right?"

I nod and tell her my appointment for that is tomorrow.

"Okay. It may still be a bit sore when you come in for chemo the next day. They'll give you instructions as to how to best care for the mediport overnight and the next morning."

She smiles and says, "You're going to be fine, Amy."

Fine? It's a funny choice of words that I've heard quite a bit lately. I don't feel fine. Nothing about this is fine.

She moves on to explain each of the four drugs, (Taxotere, Carboplatin, Herceptin, and Perjeta) I'll be receiving via my mediport IV. She slides a sheet of paper in front of Derek and me. It lists the common side effects of the premeds and chemo meds. These include:

- nausea
- diarrhea and/or constipation
- hair loss
- changes in taste
- mouth sores
- low blood counts
- peripheral neuropathy
- flu-like symptoms

Yup. All the things I've seen in the movies. This is really going to suck. But I'm doing what I need to do.

She shares ways I might manage these side effects as well as some nutrition and safety tips. When she tells me that for twenty-four hours after receiving chemo I should flush the toilet twice, I can't help but cock my head to the side, furrow my brow, and ask why.

"Small amounts of chemotherapy will be present in your bodily fluids and waste. We don't want that to come in contact with anyone else who may use the same toilet after you. It's also important you close the lid before flushing, to avoid any water splashing onto the seat."

Never would've thought of that! What is this poison I'm about to voluntarily put inside my body?

She closes the teaching session by sharing that I will receive Neulasta, a bone marrow stimulant, at the end of every treatment. The side effect of this can be bone pain, but it is very necessary in order to keep my blood counts stable.

I'm overwhelmed with all the information and feel an urge to cry. I swallow it and ask a few questions, mostly about the side effects and the meds I'll have on hand at home for these. Melissa answers each question as she slides everything into a blue folder for us to take home.

Another folder. Another stack of papers. Add it to the pile in my dresser drawer.

I still have one more box to check before chemo. Tomorrow I will have a mediport placed in my upper chest area. The port makes it easier for the nurses to administer IV chemo meds and take blood samples. This way they won't have to find veins and poke me with needles each time. Rather, they'll be able to place the needle directly into the chest port. This then allows the medication to move from the port, through the catheter in my chest, and into my bloodstream.

I've been told the port placement itself is a fairly quick procedure and, in fact, it will likely take longer to get prepped than to do the procedure. That said, I know it will still be a very emotional process. This port placement makes chemo seem more official and I know I will be starting my treatment the next day.

All the unknowns are incredibly unsettling to sit with.

What will the chemo do to me?
How will I be a mom, the way I want to be?

How will Derek and I get through this?
How will I continue to work? How will he?
Will the chemo work?

I cry my eyes out in a cathartic release. Once I can catch my breath, I turn inward and silently promise to continue showing up for myself with kindness and compassion.

I think about what Lauren told me yesterday. During healing meditations for me, she focused on my anxiety, fear, anger, and physical pain. These words came to her during the meditation:

We all have darkness. It is a balance to the light.
It is not bad. It is not good.
It is.
We are made of shadow and light.
Fear is shadow and blocks light.
Lead with love. Release fear.
You do not need to protect yourself. Just let it all flow. Fear stops flow. Love flows through all. Make space for it.

Her words help me shift my focus from fear to love, from darkness to light. She has helped me move into this next phase with more confidence in the midst of this fuckery.

CHEMO HERE WE COME (3/16/21–3/17/21)

I am terrified to start chemo tomorrow. My body writhes with anxiety over all the unknowns. Deep breathing and grounding exercises help a little, but the fear is still too loud. My parents try talking to me about various cancer-related things, such as how long chemo should take tomorrow and future appointment dates, and I get so agitated and short-tempered. I know they have a lot of emotions around all this and my responses are not meant to intentionally hurt them. I just simply can't address their questions as they remind me of all the unknowns, which makes me even more anxious.

Today's port placement was easy, other than the emotions that came along with it and the discomfort of the damn thing, now a part of my body. I cried as I was being rolled into the surgical suite and when I started getting loopy from the anesthesia. Heather and Marie, the nurses with me, were very understanding and sympathetic. At one point all I could focus on was their colorful scrubs and clog shoes and think how comfortable they looked compared to me.

I took the pre-chemo steroid about an hour ago and will take another tonight, before treatment tomorrow. It's an oral med and it tastes absolutely horrific, like I'm swallowing metal. Suddenly, my head pounds and my eyes hurt. I call the nurse line and they tell me not to take any more doses. In addition to the massive headache, the steroid also makes me super jittery, like I am crawling out of my skin. The only thing I can do to feel better is to sleep.

I have been so grateful for the support I've received since sharing the pathology update on social media. Friends, family, acquaintances, and old coworkers have all been reaching out with encouraging, supportive messages. A few of them have gone through chemo and they've shared some tips with me. As I enter this new experience, it's nice to know I have so many people behind me, praying for me, and sending me healing energy.

My friend Rebecca has offered to do another distance Reiki for me tonight. I'm hopeful I'll be able to calm my mind some and settle down a bit. My mind, body, and soul are all craving a good night's sleep before tomorrow's wreckage begins. I lie in bed as her gentle voice tells me she will be starting now. I'm in Virginia and she is in North Carolina, yet our energetic connection is so strong it feels as if her hands are hovering over my body with warm, healing energy. I doze off a bit and about an hour later I hear her soothing voice signal she's finished. I am relaxed and hopeful for a deep slumber.

I wake up and the nervousness is still present, but I also feel confident. Unfortunately, I did not sleep more than a few hours, but I am ready to take this step and kill any cancer residing in my body. Mom helps me shower and dress before I head downstairs for a light breakfast of oatmeal and fruit. I try to eat, but between my anxious belly and jumpy nerves (which the steroid hasn't helped), my stomach is hardly interested in this food. I know it will help with the nausea, though, so I force it in. I want to avoid any vomiting I can.

Andrew and Jacob are also eating breakfast and getting ready for online school. There isn't too much talking, other than in my head. In an effort to lighten the air, I try making simple conversation, but it lands flat. Zachary is hyper, zooming around the house. Childhood innocence and ignorance. He has no idea what his mom is about to endure. My focus shifts back to my older boys.

What are they thinking about all this? Do they get it? I really hope I'm not too sick afterward. I want so badly to be a good mom for them.

My chemo bag is bursting at the seams. Among other things, I'm bringing my laptop, a book, a coloring book, colored pencils, ginger candies for nausea, mala beads to help keep me calm, essential oils, and a soft, cozy blanket my parents gifted me when I was diagnosed. I hope this will allow me to feel their love and hugs all day. Derek is coming with me to this first treatment. When it's time for us to leave, we hug and kiss the boys and my parents goodbye. I hold each of my sons a little tighter and try not to cry. We step out the front door, and I turn back to give my parents one last smile with raised eyebrows, indicating, "I guess this is it. What I have to do, even though I don't want to."

It takes about twenty-five minutes to get to Dr. Ramirez's office as there is a lot of morning commute traffic. I don't think my mouth has stopped running since we got in the car. It's all nervous energy and the steroids at work. My phone dings several times on the way there with messages of support.

We arrive, park, and I take several deep breaths before exiting the car. The first treatment is expected to take about six hours. I'm glad we will be home before the boys get back from school.

Derek carries my bag. He's always so thoughtful about things like this. He knows I need nothing extra right now. I worry, though, that he may not be taking care of himself and his feelings, in an effort to put all his energy into me. I shirk the thought, remembering Martha, our therapist, told us we are only in charge of our own responses and feelings, not the other person's.

We take the stairs to the third floor. Anything to move this nervous, steroid-induced energy out of my body. I ring the bell at the door, and we are once again greeted by the same woman who takes our temperatures and asks a series of COVID clearance questions. I can feel her huge smile through her beautiful brown eyes, and I wish I could see her entire face without these damn face masks, which have become an everyday accessory for all. There are still so many unknowns about COVID and fear of spreading the disease is high, especially among immunocompromised individuals, such as chemotherapy patients. Me.

My phone dings with a text from Layton.

"Love you, love you! Here to text or chat while you sit during your appointment if you need an ear."

Before I have a chance to respond, I'm called back to the infusion suite, which is through a different door than we entered for my appointment with Dr. Ramirez. This reminds me of a pediatrician's office where they have two separate waiting rooms. One is for the "healthy" kids, the other the "sick" kids, in an effort to contain the sick germs. Is the chemo so toxic it has to be separated from the rest of the office? It doesn't smell like sickness in here. The air is light and I feel a lot of positive energy.

"I'm Ebony, one of the medical assistants, and I'll be helping your nurses today."

I appreciate her upbeat voice. One thing I don't want is for it to feel completely drab and down here. She has me step on the scale, which I absolutely hate! I have never owned a scale, as I never want to know my weight. (Body issues?) From there, we are led to my personal bay. There's a lot in this space, that seems to be about eight-by-ten feet. I glance around and see a recliner for me, a chair for Derek, the IV pole I'll be hooked up to, and some drawers, which I assume hold medical supplies.

The recliner is covered in brown vinyl and has pop-up tables on either side. Ebony shows me it has a remote to control heat and massage functions.

"It's like a pedicure chair," I joke.

I make myself at home in the recliner and Derek makes his way into the standard doctor's office chair across from me. Ebony is taking my vitals when another woman comes in to the bay.

"Hi, Amy! I'm Maria and I'll be one of your nurses today. Sara, another nurse, will also be helping out today. We want to make sure you are as comfortable as you can be. How are you feeling about today?"

Do I say, "Okay," or do I tell her how I'm really feeling?

"I'm really jittery. Both from anxiety of the unknowns and also the steroid."

After confirming my full name and birth date, I fill her in on why I didn't take the dose last night. She types notes into my electronic medical chart and talks to me at the same time.

"It's totally normal to be nervous. We're here to make sure everything goes well. Please let us know if there's anything we can do to make it any easier for you."

I nod and a whisper of, "Okay," comes out.

She then asks a series of questions regarding my health today. Her questions cover almost every part of my body, and she makes sure I'm feeling okay.

I wonder how many rounds of chemo it might take before I'm not well and my answers change here?

Today I'm healthy, other than cancer I suppose, so she hands me a cup with my Tylenol and Benadryl. She warns me the Benadryl makes most people sleepy.

"I sure hope that's the case. Between not sleeping last night and this, I should have a nice nap here."

"Me too," pipes up Derek with a smirk on his face.

Sometimes I can't tell when he's being sarcastic or serious. This is one of those times. I chuckle, showing I believe it to be a joke.

I throw back my water, and just like that, I feel as if it's officially begun. As Maria hangs medicine bags from the IV pole, I realize it would be a good idea to go to the bathroom before I'm all hooked up. I let her know I have to pee and she points to the bathroom right across the hall.

I remember to flush a second time. I wash my hands, take a deep breath, and return to my home for the day.

A VERY LONG DAY (3/17/21)

My port was left accessed yesterday, which means they won't have to stick it with a needle at all today. It's prepped and ready to be hooked up to the IV. Seeing Maria do all this is an out-of-body experience, as if I'm watching her treat someone else. She explains each step as she moves along and makes small talk, asking questions about our family, kids, work, etc. The saline drip has been going for some time now and she's lining up various syringes on the table. Because of my reaction to the steroid at home, Dr. Ramirez has instructed to skip the steroid premed as well.

"Can I get you anything? A warm blanket, pillow, water, or coffee?" Ebony asks.

I appreciate the distraction and let her know I'd love some water, and she asks Derek the same. Everyone is so kind here. The care makes it all a bit more tolerable. I recline in the chair and try to find some level of comfort.

Maria lets me know it's time for the antinausea premed and warns me some people do not like the taste. She injects it into my IV slowly and, whew, is she right! This shit tastes awful and my stomach becomes unsettled.

The medicine to prevent nausea from chemo is making me nauseated? That's some irony for you!

"That taste should go away shortly. Try drinking some water to help it."

With time the horrific taste subsides and it's time for another flush of saline.

Even though we learned about all these premeds during the teaching appointment, taking them all still seems like so much. And, because they have to do a saline flush in between each med, it seems to take forever before we even start the actual chemo meds.

My eyes flutter as the Benadryl kicks in and begins making me sleepy. Maria, Ebony, and Sara move in and out of my bay, checking on me in between premeds and checking on their other patients.

There is a chill in the air, the sound of people talking in their own bays, and a lot of machines beeping. Every time a bag of medicine finishes dripping, the machine attached to it (for measuring and monitoring the flow) emits this incessant beeping sound. The beep continues until someone presses a magic button on the machine. With the number of people receiving chemo today and the different meds running at different rates, the beeping seems to be steady in the background.

Maria and Sara return. After asking how I'm doing, Maria reaches into one of the drawers. She pulls out a medical gown of sorts and what looks like a present wrapped in tissue paper without the bow. She puts the gown on, on top of her scrubs. She carefully opens the package on her table and I can see it contains gloves, masks, and alcohol wipes. On the table also lies a big IV bag filled with what I assume is my first chemo med, Carboplatin.

Why is she wearing that? Why is she putting an extra mask and two layers of gloves on?

I'm so curious that I ask and she explains it's to protect her from Carboplatin should it touch her. She downplays it, explaining they wear the gown and extra gloves in case of a spill, but it's very unlikely to happen. She reminds me that today each of the meds will be delivered at a slower rate, to be sure I don't have any allergic reactions. Carboplatin and Taxotere will each take one and a half hours; Herceptin and Perjeta will each take an hour. Assuming all goes well, these times will be reduced at my next session.

"Can you please tell us your full name and birth date?" Maria kindly asks.

"Amy Michelle Banocy. 5/5/77."

Maria repeats my name and birthday and then rattles off a bunch of numbers I suppose are associated with my patient account. She reads aloud the name and dose of medicine off the bag, the rate at which it will drip and for how long, and another long number. Derek and I look at each other as if to say, "What the fuck?" As she's reciting all this information, Sara is confirming it matches what is on the screen in front of her. Any mismatches and they start over. This is to ensure everything Dr. Ramirez has ordered for me is what is actually given to me. Once matched, she hangs the bag of meds and we're off.

Carboplatin is now entering my body. I am receiving chemotherapy drugs. Despite having just stated my name and birth date, it still does not connect that I am truly here, attempting to kill any cancer in my body.

I'm smiling and just taking what she gives me, without any thought as to what is happening on the inside.

Maria tells me to call for a nurse if I feel anything unusual, such as nausea, dizziness, headache, or itching. I'm listening but I just want to sleep.

Less than two minutes have gone by when a wave of nausea washes over me. Thinking it'll pass, I don't say anything at first. It comes again, this time more intensely.

Shit. I'm going to throw up.

"I'm really nauseated and hot. I feel like I'm going to throw up," I say as quickly as I can. Sara hands me a blue, plastic vomit bag. It's the same as the one I held close to my mouth after surgery. She stops the Carboplatin.

I'm dizzy and queasy, and I just want to close my eyes and not feel this. Fear rises within me.

Maria returns and both nurses are on top of the situation at hand. They ask me how I'm doing and assure me the nausea should pass quickly now the medicine has been stopped.

My eyes glance over at Derek. He looks as afraid as I feel. I'm glad he's here, for me. For him, I wish he didn't have to witness any of this.

"Can you pass me my oils please?" I ask Derek. He hands them to me and I quickly take the cap off the peppermint, lower my mask, and bring it up to my nose.

I'm given some additional nausea meds and the nurses have been given the go ahead from Dr. R to try the Carboplatin again, at an even slower dosing rate, once the shitty feelings subside. My stomach is unsettled with some slight nausea but I muster through.

Derek tries to get some work done on his laptop. I try to sleep, but I just can't. My body is filled with conflicting feelings of fatigue and hyper-alertness. Random thoughts keep popping in my head about the kids, our schedule, or my parents. The thoughts exit my mouth and lead to brief conversations between us. I take out my coloring book and colored pencils, out of boredom and a desire to take my mind off the waves rolling in my belly. Shades of purple, green, and yellow fill in the beautiful mandala on the page.

The nurses and Ebony continue checking on me and offering items of comfort. Rounds of water continue to be delivered upon request. Naturally, I need to use the bathroom. I'm attached to the IV pole which is plugged into the wall.

Can I unplug it? Will it stop running? I don't want to bother anyone by asking. I'll just wait until they come back. It can't be that long.

I'm right and moments later Maria is back. She checks the bag hanging from the pole and tells me I have about fifteen minutes of Carboplatin remaining. One side effect of Taxotere is neuropathy. To prevent this, I'll hold ice packs in my hands and keep my feet on another—before, during, and after Taxotere is administered. She's holding two frozen water bottles, a pair of white gloves, and a larger ice pack. Before she can explain, I ask about using the bathroom.

"Oh yes! Of course you can unplug. I'm so sorry I didn't let you know before. Everything will continue to run on the battery."

I cautiously shuffle across the hall as I maneuver the pole, the cords, and my body. While washing my hands, I can't help but stare at my reflection in the mirror.

Who is this woman? This is not me. This is not real.

Tears gather in the corners of my eyes. I splash my face with some water, take a few deep breaths, and exit the bathroom.

"You okay, babe?" Derek can tell I've washed the tears away.

"Yeah. I think so."

I take my seat, recline a little, and wait for Maria.

She's back in a flash and gives me thin white gloves and a

frozen water bottle to hold in each hand. They're so cold it sends a shiver down my spine.

"You'll need to sit up for this part, so your feet can reach the ice pack on the floor."

Like a good student, I follow her instructions. I place my feet on the ice pack. It is absolutely freezing. I pull my feet back and Maria asks if I brought an extra pair of socks. Nope. Didn't know to do that. Next time I'll bring my warm, fuzzy socks. For now, I put my feet back on the ice and accept the offer for a warm blanket.

"Is that okay, Amy?"

I nod, even though I'm uncomfortable. I know I don't have a choice, so I go with it.

"Okay. You'll keep the ice on for the remainder of the Carbo, throughout the Taxotere, and about fifteen to twenty minutes after that finishes."

I do the math in my head. About two hours of this biting cold.

Maria leaves the bay and I glance at Derek, shake the water bottles, and giggle. He snaps a picture to capture the jovial moment. Nobody will see the moments when I feel afraid, sick, or helpless. I will push these feelings to the back of my mind, only to live in my subconscious.

Beep.

I made it through Carboplatin. It feels like we've been here all day. I'm exhausted and we still have so much left to do.

I receive texts from so many wonderful people throughout the day. Layton's name appears in my text notifications and I am reminded I never responded to her earlier text.

"Bestie check-in time!"

"Long day but going okay! Thanks for checking in."

"Of course and I bet. But all done and home now? Feel free to ignore if you are resting/with peeps/whatever else!"

"Oh no…won't be home for *hours!*"

"Shows how much I know. Can you eat? Do you have snacky snacks?"

Her comment makes me realize I am a bit hungry, so I ask Derek to pass my bag over and I grab my pretzels. With my dietary restrictions, one thing I've learned is to bring my own food to appointments, hospitals, and chemo.

Maria, Sara, and Ebony are incredibly compassionate and attentive. I am very well taken care of, which brings a special kind of tenderness.

Taxotere goes well, and while I'm receiving the Herceptin an "Artist in Residence" comes around with a cart full of art supplies. He introduces himself as Steve and is so incredibly warm and friendly. After some small talk, he turns to his cart and asks if we'd like to do a craft.

"It's a nice way to pass the time while you're here. You can paint one of these wooden signs, color, or make a collage. I have tons of magazines and you can make it as big or small as you want. Look at what other people have done."

After showing us the collages, I say, "Sure. I'll make one."

Derek accepts a wooden sign and some paint.

Steve chats with us as we get started and then tells us he will check back in a bit. We hear him visiting other patients' bays, introducing himself with the same vibrant, cheerful voice.

Derek, being the artist of the family, takes to the idea of crafting. I am a bit more hesitant and really just do it to keep my mind off what is really going on. I slowly cut pages out of the magazines. I cut out positive affirmations, inspirational words, and pictures. I rub the glue stick on the page and try not to worry about perfection.

Surprisingly, I find this craft relaxing. Steve returns and we inquire more about his being here.

"Each day of the week someone comes in from the Living with Cancer organization. Sometimes an artist or a musician or a counselor. We help provide creative outlets, relaxation, and support for patients and caregivers," he shares as he moves papers around on his art cart.

"Wow! That's really amazing! I love this idea," I glance up from my project and reply.

Both Herceptin and Perjeta seem to finish quickly. After that it's Neulasta and finally the process of deaccessing my port.

Ten hours after walking in the door, we finally walk out. I am completely drained, physically and mentally. I assume Derek is as well. As we walk to the car, I feel so thankful Derek came with me. He not only served as support for me but also as a second set of ears and eyes to all that was happening. Plus, it was nice to have that time together, away from kids and the hustle of everyday life. Not the best circumstances to spend this time together, but I think we both appreciated it nonetheless.

I reach for his hand, hold it, and squeeze.

"Thank you for being here with me today."

"Babe. I'll always be here for you. No matter what."

One down, five to go. I'll be back in that chair in another three weeks, on April 7, 2021.

I doze on the ride home, drifting in and out of thought and wondering what these next few weeks will be like.

THE WEEKS IN BETWEEN

I barely make it to the next day before the nausea hits. A few minutes before midnight I wake up feeling queasy and head to the bathroom. On the counter sits all my meds, neatly organized in a plastic caddy, like candies to be grabbed à la carte. I pop a Zofran Melt and, as it sits on my tongue, I try to ignore the chalky flavor the box labels "strawberry." I say a little prayer it will do the trick and I'll be able to go back to sleep. I'm so tired; I consider nausea one of the worst feelings and I have a strange fear around vomiting. I hate it. I feel like I won't be able to breathe and it will never cease.

I wake up and glance at the clock to see it is 5 a.m. I must've fallen asleep somewhere around 1 a.m. because I don't remember seeing the clock after then until now. In addition to feeling sick to my stomach, my face is now very flushed. I use every bit of energy I have to reach over to my bedside table for a few pretzels and water. I eat the small pretzels incredibly slowly, nibble by nibble. I am aware of the crunching sound they make and don't want to wake Derek, so I take a little nibble and let it soften and dissolve in my mouth. This also allows me to savor every grain of salt.

I slowly head downstairs for a cup of tea. I am not a tea drinker, other than when I am sick, which I believe this qualifies as. Trust me, I'd much rather have a cup of coffee, but my stomach is telling me otherwise. Several of the gift packages I've received have included boxes of tea, so I've accumulated a nice stash. Like combing through a file drawer, I look at the tea selections and land on citrus-ginger. Not because it sounds good but because it sounds like it's going to help me feel better.

The next few hours are much of the same. Wake. Nausea. Zofran. Water. Tea.

My stomachache evolves into this weird mix of feelings like I'm going to have diarrhea or be gassy or maybe even constipated. I know they are typically all very different feelings, but I'm experiencing a mixture of all of them at once. Part of this is probably because a side effect of the Zofran is constipation. I also feel urinary pressure and wonder what that is all about, especially since I've been drinking a lot of water.

"How are you doing, babe?" Derek asks when he wakes up.

I shrug my shoulders. "I feel like shit. I've been up during the night and have been taking meds for the nausea. I'm going to try and fall asleep again. And I'm really achy, but don't know if that's from the chemo, the Neulasta, or my fibromyalgia. Who knows?"

The day consists of sleeping, waking, trying to eat small bites, feeling ill, and taking a lot of medicines. When I do make it downstairs, I feel like a zombie, moving in slow motion. Mom and Dad are there to help out with the kids while Derek is working.

"Hi, sweet girl. How are you feeling?" Mom pops up from her seat on the couch.

I manage to pull out the closest chair at the table and sit.

"Derek told us you didn't sleep well. Has the nausea gotten any better? Can I get you anything?"

A wave of nausea rolls in. I swallow hard and tell her I don't think I can eat but I'll try. I attempt some toast and coffee. I am unsuccessful. I just can't. With every bite, I think I'm going to throw up.

I have a clear view of Zachary sitting at his makeshift school desk, attending virtual school. I smile at the sight and sound of my youngest child. He comes over and gives me a great big hug and asks me how I'm feeling.

I don't want this for him. I don't want him to worry, but I also know I cannot hide the truth of this.

"I'm really not feeling good today, Z. Thank you for asking. I'm actually going to go back upstairs and sleep more. Have a great rest of the school day, buddy. I love you," I reply as I give him another big hug and kiss.

By evening I've added Colace for constipation, Tylenol for headache, and Promethazine for nausea into the mix of meds. I'm upstairs as I hear my family gather around the table to enjoy a delicious meal someone has delivered. I long to be able to enjoy it all, the food and the company. The boys have each come in to hug me and snuggle me throughout the day and do so once more before going to bed. I am so grateful for moments of connection with my kids despite or because of my illness.

The next day is a rerun of the same show. Go downstairs, try to eat a little bit of oatmeal or toast in the morning, spend maybe ten to fifteen minutes there, go back to sleep for four to five more hours, try to eat again, and then sleep again. The exhaustion from chemo is like nothing else I've ever experienced. Not even those long-ago nights filled with nursing a newborn have anything on this. The exhaustion is deep in my bones. I can't focus. My feet shuffle along the floor when I walk. My words come out in mumbles. Even when I do not want to sleep, I do not have a choice. My body finds its way back into bed and my eyes close within seconds.

I want to take a walk. I crave the outdoors. But I can't do it. I'm too tired. Too queasy. Too uncomfortable. I want to be doing, but know my body needs the rest. And while I know this, I still hate feeling so tired!

I am also plagued with the horrible cycle of diarrhea and constipation. I've been in touch with Dr. Ramirez and Melissa about this, and we're hoping I can figure out the right mix of things to be somewhat regular.

I'm cheered up a bit by the numerous texts and calls from friends and family checking in on me.

Day five brings me a little more energy and I'm able to take a thirty-minute walk. It feels so good to be outside and move my body, albeit quite slowly.

I've developed this weird fuzzy feeling on my tongue. It has become harder to eat solid foods, so I drink a lot of smoothies.

Today I am scheduled to receive my COVID-19 vaccine. I've heard about some of the flu-like side effects and jokingly say to my parents, "Well, I guess I won't know if it's chemo or the vaccine causing it!"

Although my energy is up, I still look like hell. My eyelids droop, my face sags, and the nosebleeds I've been having have me walking around with a tissue pressed to my nose almost constantly. So, I notice the stares as I walk in for the vaccine.

Do they think I have COVID? Should I say something?

I choose to ignore it and wait my place in line, and the vaccine goes off without an issue. It feels really great to be out of the house with my mom. I feel a little more relaxed and normal, even if just for this brief time.

My sister Leigh meets us back at the house, and I'm happy to see her. She has been amazing, driving nearly an hour each way to visit almost every day. She tells me she just wants to be with me, whether I'm sleeping most of the time she's around or not. She's also been a great support system for my parents and the boys. Today we enjoy acai bowls and time out on my deck with mom and dad. The company, the cool flavor of the acai, and the fresh air all feel great.

I wonder what it's like to witness your baby sister going through all this shit. I'm so fucking lucky to have her!

My diarrhea has worsened. Tonight, I actually Google "yoga moves to stop diarrhea" and, believe it or not, there is a suggestion. I lie on the floor with my butt edged up against the wall and straighten out my legs, so they are on the wall. I stay in this position as suggested and then I return to bed. My stomach rumbles and I know the feeling all too well. Unfortunately, the yoga pose didn't work for me. Maybe tomorrow I'll look into more exercises. For now, I rush back into the bathroom.

Do I take more Imodium? I am hesitant because I don't want to constipate myself and continue in the cycle again.

While I am experiencing these side effects and feel miserable, the fact that I am getting chemo still doesn't feel real. It's like I went there and got this treatment, but it wasn't really me in that chair. Almost like I removed my actual self from the experience and only my body was there. I suppose that is survival mode and a lot of denial at play.

I am also really struggling with feeling useless at home, and anger is setting in. I don't want to be around the family. I retreat to my room more often. I hate asking for help and put it off until it is absolutely necessary. I try to push away these feelings by doing yoga and walking outside. Fresh air seems to help, but I am still pissed off.

Why me? What did I do to deserve this? I'm a good person.

I make it through another night and cry as I attempt to sip my morning coffee the next day. My stomach just will not allow it. Through the tears, I say to my parents, "I can't even drink my fucking coffee!" My dad hugs me and I melt into his arms.

What is my life becoming?

I have moments of relief and take the opportunity to get outside when I can. I sit on the front step and watch the boys play basketball or I go for a walk with them. I stretch and attempt to do light yoga when I'm able.

Despite those respites, I spend much of the time feeling useless, lost, and so tired. And I know I am only one mile into this chemo marathon.

Tonight we will celebrate Zachary's eighth birthday with an outdoor movie, popcorn, and cake. Between COVID protocols and cancer, this kid is ready for a party with his friends. From the moment he wakes up he is so excited, which makes me smile.

Later, as I stand at the table cutting slices of pizza for the kids, a wave of nausea hits. I put down the pizza slicer and quickly, but quietly, make my way inside. I don't want to make a scene. I don't want anyone to follow me. I just want to get some water, sit, and hope the feeling passes as quickly as it came on. It does, and I don't think anyone noticed me missing.

By the time we're serving cake, I am completely exhausted. Not only from standing as much as I have but also from the social interaction. It's exhausting answering, "How are you doing?" what seems like a hundred times. But I answer every time because I appreciate the care and concern and do not want to be rude.

The birthday party has turned into a bit of a neighborhood block party. All our neighbors are outside. Kids are indulging in cake, and adults indulge in beverages of the alcoholic variety. I'm overcome with envy and sadness. I love block parties and I'm mad I can't enjoy this one. I've lasted as long as I can out here and know it's time for me to head to bed. Before going in, I head over to Z.

"I'm going to bed, bud. I hope you had fun tonight."

"Are you not feeling well?"

"No, I'm okay. I'm just really tired."

As I lean down to kiss him, he says, "This was the best night, Mom. Thank you!"

I squeeze him in a tight hug, using all the energy I have left, and head inside.

A few days ago my parents suggested Derek and I go to the beach for a couple of days, if I feel up for it, while they're here. Knowing I'll be back in that brown recliner in a little more than a week, I jumped—well, not literally—at the opportunity. Even if I feel like shit, I'd rather it be at the beach!

We found an adorable little bungalow to rent and will head there today. I begin packing after breakfast and, as I collect my toiletries and such, I'm reminded of a new reality. Oh, the meds I have to bring! Not only the meds I have to take but also the "just in case" ones. I do not want to be that far away and not have what I might need. Colace for the constipation.

Fiber mix to help get things going. Imodium in case it turns to diarrhea. Zofran and Phenergan in case of nausea. As I load medication after medication into a bag, cancer is right here in my face. I plop down on my bed, scream into a pillow, and kick my legs. I'm fuming, yet I know I have a choice. I can decide not to go because it is too much or I can go and try to enjoy the time away.

I sleep most of the three-hour drive there. After finding the house and dropping off our stuff, we head to the beach before it gets dark. Despite the cooler temp, I immediately take my shoes off. I sit there, staring out into the water. I walk down to the water and dip my toes in. The freeze immediately reminds me of the ice bags at chemo and I walk back to my chair. Derek reaches for my hand and gives it a squeeze.

"I love you, babe," he says with a little smile.

"I love you too. I'm glad we did this. It feels good to be away."

In moments like these, it's as if our recent very rocky past didn't exist.

Are we really fine now or has cancer simply taken over and we are in survival mode? What will it be like after cancer? Will we go back to therapy and pick up where we left off, or will we just move on from here because things are more back to normal for us now?

With the temp dropping and the wind picking up, we decide it's time to pack up the chairs and grab some dinner. We find a cute beachy restaurant, complete with hammocks and Adirondack chairs, and I'm in heaven. Well, almost. I just want to sit here and enjoy a nice glass of wine and some good food. My stomach isn't quite on board, though, and once again this causes some sadness and anger.

"I just want to enjoy a fucking glass of wine."

"Get one and see if you can drink it. If not, no big deal. Or if you don't want to, I won't get anything to drink either."

"No, you get a beer. I'll be fine. At least one of us should enjoy."

I mean this in the nicest way yet I realize it comes out with a snarky tone. It's how my feelings show themselves.

The next day, I feel a bit less lethargic and suggest we walk around the town. We pop in and out of stores, window-shop a bit, and try to find a place that serves dairy-free ice cream.

"Derek, I'm exhausted now. I need a nap."

"Okay. I was hoping to do that walk I mentioned earlier. I'd really like to see that area. Are you okay if I go while you nap?"

I encourage him to go, and he heads out after dropping me off at the bungalow.

When I hear the door to the cottage open, I don't know how long I've been asleep. It seems like I've been asleep for hours, and checking the time on my phone confirms this.

Derek cuddles up to me in bed. I feel some hesitation in my body, but I go with the flow.

He's so good to me. How can I turn away from him now?

He kisses me and I kiss him right back. In my mind, that'll be it. Some cuddles and kisses. He has different plans and for some reason thinks it's time for us to make out.

I push back.

"I'm sorry. I just don't want to. I'm not feeling it."

He looks completely defeated.

"Do you not feel well or do you not feel like making out with me?"

"A bit of both I guess."

I do not want to have this conversation right now.

He's visibly upset.

"I can understand not feeling up for it because of chemo, but I don't understand if it's other reasons. It seems like things have been really good with us. Am I wrong?"

I can't do this now. I don't have the energy.

"I really don't want to talk about this right now. I don't have the energy or headspace. Can we just watch a show or something and have our leftovers for dinner?"

He acquiesces and I begin to get up from the bed when an

awful feeling in my stomach arises. Is it the conversation or has the fiber drink finally kicked in? I make my way downstairs. He follows. We have a quiet night and go to bed without further addressing the situation.

Upon waking the next morning, I lie in bed and wonder whether we had two very different ideas for this time away. I hoped for rest, relaxation, and healing. But it seems Derek wanted more closeness and connection.

Why don't I want the same? I should want that. As always, I enjoy the time together, but I'm struggling with this piece of it. Is it because of how I feel physically, or do I still not feel that connection?

I push the emotions away and head downstairs to shower. We're planning to go out for breakfast before heading back home. I begin to cry in the shower. All the thoughts that were running through my mind this morning are still there. I wash my face and, with it, the tears. It's only the beginning of my tears in this shower, though.

My hair started to thin and become looser about a week after my first chemo treatment, and little pieces have been coming out here and there. As I shampoo my hair, I notice the first real clump of hair has come out in my hands. I stand there crying, frozen in time, this mound of hair in my hands. I feel disgusted and powerless, so I quickly finish my shower. Before getting out, I look down at the drain, where more of my long, beautiful hair lies.

I wrap a towel around myself, grab the hair with a few tissues, and toss it in the trash can. I stand there for a moment, paralyzed by my anger and sadness.

"Derek, can you come here please?" I call, my voice quivering.

He stands in the doorway of the bathroom as I manage to mumble, "Look," and point to the trash can, which visibly contains my hair.

The tears spill out.

My body is shaking.

My fear of losing my hair is happening and I have zero control over it.

"I don't want to lose my fucking hair. I don't want to be bald. Now everyone is going to know I have cancer. People are going to look at me like some kind of cancer patient. I don't want it! I don't want this! Cancer is taking yet another thing from me. It's not fair!" I scream through my tears.

He wraps me in a hug. "I know, babe. I know. It fucking sucks. You're going to be beautiful no matter what. I know you may not want to hear that right now. It's the truth and what I know, though."

I continue to cry. He continues to hug me. I step back and thank him.

I grab a tissue, as I feel my nose running from all the crying. Nope—it's another nosebleed.

Here I stand: in the bathroom, towel wrapped around me, constipated, my hair beginning to fall out, and with a nosebleed.

This is cancer.

This is chemo.

This is my new reality.

HAIR TODAY, GONE TOMORROW

―

When I was told I'd need to undergo chemotherapy, I immediately thought about my hair and the fear of losing it. These long, curly brown locks, gone? I dreaded the day! Not only because I didn't want to be bald but also because I felt it would make me "look" like a cancer patient. I was afraid of what it would mean to have my cancer be visible to others. Losing my breasts seemed like a more drastic loss, but it was also one I could keep hidden. With tissue expanders, nobody could tell the difference.

Will people stare at me? Will kids see me and ask their parents why I don't have hair? Will people treat me differently?

My hair. My long, beautiful, curly hair. I love my hair. I love that I can make it curly or straight depending on my mood. I love that I can change the style, the color, and the length, and that I have done so often.

My hair, that has grown with me since birth, is now going to be taken from me. Without my permission.

I know it is just hair. I know I can sport some fun wigs or hats if I choose to. I know it will grow back. These things do not matter when this impending loss is so present.

I shared these thoughts and fears in last week's group therapy session.

As soon as I finished speaking, Dan, one of the wise men in the group, said, "Amy, you're not going to look like a cancer patient. You're going to look like a fucking badass!"

I heard that and immediately felt butterflies in my stomach, chills on my body, and a huge fucking smile on my face. Tears ran down my face at this encouragement and reminder that I control the narrative in my head, and by changing the story, I can shift how I view and feel about the situation at hand.

I'm going to look like a fucking badass!
I'm going to look like a fucking badass!
I'm going to look like a fucking badass!

Since that day, I've been telling myself this phrase over and over, especially when I look in the mirror. It has become somewhat of an affirmation for me.

My hair has continued to fall out in the days following the beach, and I want to take control. I think it will be less drastic for me if I cut my hair short before possibly losing it all completely. I reach out to my hair girl Natalie and share my thoughts. She immediately texts me back.

"Hey! That's a really good idea! Will Derek be able to be there? I think it helps having loved ones around for this next step. I've done this for one other friend, and she had a little party with her close friends. Everyone got to cut a little bit and it made it a better experience."

I love the idea of being surrounded by love and my favorite humans in the world, turning this scary moment into a celebration.

I tell Derek about the plan, and he asks what I think about blow-drying and doing my hair tonight and taking a picture as a memory.

I'm fairly certain he is more aware of how this upcoming loss is going to affect me than I am. I am exhausted after doing my hair and am also so glad for this moment. I know I'm going to want to have this picture to look back at someday and I'm grateful Derek had the thought.

It's March 31 and my hair is about to be cut the shortest that it has ever been by far. I'm very emotional. Derek, my three sweet boys, my parents, and Layton are here with me, as well as my sister Leigh and nieces, Lauren and Sarah, joining us on FaceTime. After hugs all around, Natalie gives me a hug and whispers, "Okay, you ready?"

I take a deep breath, wipe my tears, and sit down in her chair. It's a chair I've sat in many times. Never ever did I think I'd be here for this purpose.

"You're going to be beautiful! And we're going to have so much fun with it when it grows back. I promise!" Natalie says, with love in her eyes.

The soft bristles of her brush move through my hair. Over and over again.

I won't feel this for a long time.

After separating my hair into eight ponytails, she turns to my party squad and says, "Anyone who wants to will have a chance to cut one off. Does anyone want to go first?"

Everyone is frozen. It's as if someone hit pause on our movie.

"Mom. I want you to go first," somehow escapes my lips, quietly, as I turn to the right and look up at my mom.

She takes the scissors from Natalie and gives me a look of disbelief. She then bends down and gives me a kiss on the cheek, through her mask, of course.

She saw my first haircut as a baby. And now this? How is any of this fair?

Natalie directs her to cut right above the elastic hair band, and just like that one of the ponytails is now in her hand. Everyone has their phone out and is taking pictures and videos. It feels a bit like the paparazzi are here with me. She hands the hair to Natalie and asks who wants to go next. I can see her hands shaking and she's holding back tears behind her glasses.

"I'll go next," I hear coming from my left side, and I'm surprised to see it's my sweet Jacob. I wasn't sure he was going to participate in the cutting, but he walks to my mom and takes the scissors from her. He is such a sensitive soul and I wonder how all this has been affecting him. Just before cutting, he triple-checks he's doing it right. This makes me think he's nervous. He cuts and another ponytail is off.

"My turn," I hear Zachary say, and he seems eager to take the scissors from Jacob. He selects the ponytail of his liking. Derek holds it for him and he begins cutting. He has some trouble, as the hair is thicker than he anticipated.

"Sorry, Amy," Derek jokes, and everyone gets a chuckle out of it. Z finishes and the ponytail falls into Derek's hand.

Andrew steps up next and breaks the record for the fastest ponytail chop off so far.

I glance at the ponytails lined up on Natalie's workstation. Four down.

Derek takes the scissors next. I glance at his reflection in the mirror and see this man who will do anything for me. The man I married nearly twenty years ago, in sickness and in health. The scissors move through the ponytail, and when it lands in his hand, he leans over, kisses my head, and gives my shoulders a little squeeze.

Ponytail number five joins the others and Derek hands the scissors to my dad.

Oh, Daddy. This is just too much.

At six-foot-four, he is towering over me. I glance up at him and immediately I am his little girl again. My dad is unlike any other out there. He is kind, compassionate, emotional, and tenderhearted.

"This is not easy to do. You know?" he says as he gently takes a ponytail in his left hand, the scissor in his right.

"Daddy, I love you."

"This was not on the list of the things I was supposed to do as a dad," he says as he chokes back tears.

He cuts through the hair, places it with the others, and kisses me on the forehead.

This leaves Layton. We have been through so many of life's ups and downs together. For me, it was a given she must be here with me tonight. I can't imagine not having her witness and participate in this.

"You ready, beautiful?" she says as she steps up to my head.

I nod, with tears in my eyes.

With gentle, shaky hands, she cuts the ponytail and then leans down and kisses my head. I notice she runs her hand over the ponytail before handing it to Natalie.

Dear G-d, please never let me have to go through this for anyone else here.

One ponytail remains. Since my sister and nieces are out of town, I told her I'd cut one for both her and me. It's really hard not having her here and I would've waited for her to be back in town if the hair hadn't been falling out so quickly. This cut will have to do for the both of us. My mom has had Leigh, Lauren, and Sarah on FaceTime this entire time. She brings the phone closer to me.

Natalie pulls the final ponytail and holds it out, to make room for me to cut it.

"This is hard to do looking in a mirror. Are the scissors around it?" I say, laughing nervously.

This is it, Amy. Take a minute before you cut.

"You got it, Amy," I hear, but am unsure who said it. It truly doesn't matter. I'm surrounded by so much love right now.

I slowly move the scissors through, feeling each strand of hair as it loosens from my head. With the final cut, I close my eyes and cry.

"We love you, Amy," I hear coming from several voices.

Natalie hands me all eight ponytails and I hold them on display.

"Oh my gosh! This was all on my head!"

I'm so glad this night has been captured in video and pictures. Someday, when all this cancer fuckery passes and my hair is growing back, I'll look at them and marvel at my bravery.

For now, I tilt my head forward and Natalie begins to shave it short. There's a lot of commenting as she trims. I can feel the nervous energy in the room.

She has shaved the back and underneath, but the top is still a mop. It looks like a mushroom.

"Maybe I should leave it like this?" I joke and model the look to both my left and right side.

After a few chuckles, she continues, and the closer she gets to the front the more emotional I become. I clench my fists under the cape.

Jacob gets up and hugs me over my back.

"I love you, buddy!"

"I love you too, Mom."

Natalie directs me back to the washing station. I am shaking as I walk back and take a seat.

It feels so weird as she washes my head.

I return to my seat at her station, look in the mirror, and am not sure who is staring back at me. It's like looking at a different person. I laugh because I look so much like my mom right now.

I smile.

It's not as bad as I thought it might be.

Natalie gives me some styling tips for the remaining days before we will likely need to shave it completely.

I stand up from the chair and each of my boys comes over to hug me. Then my parents and then Derek.

"You look beautiful, babe," he tells me in the hug.

"Thank you."

I vow to myself to embrace the new look. I may have never had a short cut like this if not for this cancer fuckery.

CHEMO CONTINUES

As the days go on, I slowly begin to feel human again. I feel more like myself and less like some demon has taken hold of my body. By April 2, five days before chemo round two, I'm getting out for walks, eating more, helping my kids with schoolwork, and spending more time awake with them.

Okay. I can handle this! I can do this again. I'm ready.

Our brains are at some point able to forget how hard chemo was, much like with childbirth, and we begin to think we could do it again. It's as if my mind is forgetting the previous weeks as I prepare to suit up for battle again.

Don't get me wrong, I am still anxious heading into this next round, but for different reasons. This time I know what to expect afterward and I *do not* want *any* of it! Sometimes ignorance is bliss.

Due to the reaction I had to Carboplatin during round one, Dr. Ramirez wants me to take the pre-chemo steroid again. Despite the horrible headaches I experienced last go-round, in weighing the options, she feels getting the chemo meds into my body is the priority, so we'll try the steroid again and hope both the headaches and the Carboplatin will be more tolerable.

I take the steroid the night before and morning of. I have a headache, but it's not as awful as last time.

I can stick this out. I have to stick it out.

I am beginning to have a love-hate relationship with chemotherapy—well, it may be acceptance and not love. On the one hand, I welcome the meds because they are killing the cancer. On the other, I fucking hate it! I hate the prep and what it does to my body in the days following treatment.

Today is the first time they will need to access my port, which means sticking a needle in it. As instructed, I've applied some numbing cream to the port and have covered it with Saran Wrap. This way it should be nice and numb by the time they access it.

As Derek and I head out the door, the boys give me big hugs and kisses. I squeeze each of them tightly.

"Mom, will you be tired when you get home or can we play a game together?" Zachary asks.

"I'll have to see how I feel, buddy. If we can't play today, we will definitely do it another time soon. I promise."

It breaks my heart to not know whether I'll have the energy.

Derek grabs my chemo bag, which is a bit lighter this time. With a more realistic idea of how my time will likely be spent, I've left out several things I didn't need or use last time.

Maria is my nurse again today. I really like having chemo here in Dr. Ramirez's office because it's small and seems more personal. Before starting, the other option I was given was to be treated at the main cancer center, which is much larger and has many more nurses on rotation.

Walking in today feels different. It feels good to know what to expect and the order of things. It may only be my second treatment but part of me feels like an old pro. It could be my killer short haircut giving me a confidence boost too.

After getting weighed, as we're walking to my infusion bay, I make eye contact with a few of the other patients. I've read books and watched movies where the characters became friends with other patients while undergoing chemotherapy. I wonder if this will happen for me. Most people keep their curtain open, and we nod at each other and say hello, but that is about the extent of it. I wouldn't mind meeting someone my age. I think it would be nice to have someone to go through all this with. Someone who really understands.

"Your hair looks so cute like that! And I really like your mask. The sunflowers are very cheery," the medical assistant says, looking at me while taking my vitals.

I smile under my mask, even though she can't see it.

It's cold here today, so I wear the super soft, fuzzy cardigan one of my mom's friends sent me.

Things start off much like last time. The medical assistant asks me a series of questions about how I'm feeling and how I've been over the past three weeks. We discuss my battle with constipation and diarrhea, and I tell her I think I've gotten it under control and I've figured out the right amounts of the different meds to try if I need to this time around. She mentions a registered dietitian will be here today and will likely stop by.

"Is there anything I can get for you to help make you more comfortable? Pillow? Warm blanket?"

I let her know I'm fine and Maria walks in as she finishes up. It's so nice to see her friendly and familiar face. With as many routine questions as there are to answer and information to repeat in general, I appreciate my experience with the first treatment doesn't have to be retold.

"So, because of the reaction you had to it last time, Dr. Ramirez wants us to run the Carboplatin slowly again. We're all pretty confident you'll be fine this time since you took the steroid, but we just want to be sure," she says while prepping my premeds.

I give a nod in recognition. "Better safe than sorry."

I swallow down the oral premeds as Maria prepares to access my port.

My tank top is covering part of the port and she asks me to hold it down just a little bit.

"Did you numb your port this morning?"

"Yes, about an hour ago," I respond with a thumbs up.

"Perfect. You shouldn't feel much more than a pinch."

I continue to hold my tank out of the way as she cleanses the area. She wipes it three times and then sterilizes it.

"I'm going to count to three and on three you'll feel a little pinch. Take a deep breath for me. One, two, three…"

Pinch!

"Alright. Great job. We'll go ahead and get started with your other premeds and then we'll get going with the chemo. You feel alright?" she says as she secures the needle and tubing with what looks like a large Band-Aid.

"Yup. Doing good. Thanks," and this time I mean it. I do feel good. I feel like I'm crushing my chemo game so far today!

The premeds all go well and Maria is now putting the medical gown on top of her scrubs. She calls for another nurse to come check the info for my chemo.

"Can you please tell us your full name and birth date?" she begins.

"Amy Michelle Banocy. 5/5/77."

Like a robot, she repeats the information back and reads a long series of numbers. The other nurse confirms it's all correct, just like last time.

I take a deep breath as she hangs the bag of Carboplatin from the IV pole.

"Okay, Amy. Let us know right away if you feel anything off. Nausea, itching, or pain. Anything. You let us know."

"Yup. Let's hope that's not the case," I say as I exhale and cross my fingers.

She agrees and asks me again if I need anything before she steps out.

I tell her no, and then it's just Derek and me there.

We pass the time switching between chatting and reading our books. Both Maria and the assistant check on me every so often. After a while I start to get sleepy, but Maria comes in holding ice bottles just as I'm reclining the chair to hopefully rest.

"Time to start the fun part," she says with a hint of joking in her tone.

I sit back up and Derek passes me the warm, fuzzy socks I remembered to bring this time.

Socks and gloves on. Feet resting on ice pack on the floor and hands holding frozen water bottles.

This better work! I hope I'm not doing this for nothing.

It isn't much longer before the beep, beep, beep sounds. I have successfully made it through my second round of Carboplatin! And no major nausea this time. This is definitely a win.

Once again, I'm asked for my name and birth date. And, once again, a series of numbers are rattled off and confirmed by a second nurse.

The dietitian stops by when Taxotere has slowly been dripping into my body for some time.

"Hi, Amy. My name is Deb and I'm one of the registered dietitians here. I heard you had some issues with diarrhea and constipation after your first chemo and I'm here to help you figure out how you can avoid that. So, tell me what's been going on."

I share the details of the past three weeks, ending with the fact that I think I've figured it out.

"Oh, wonderful! Some things to consider are making sure you're staying hydrated and getting enough protein. Do you have any protein drinks like this one?" she says, lifting up a bottle.

"I use a plant-based protein powder in my shakes with fruit and spinach every morning. I've been trying to keep up with this, but sometimes I'm just too tired to make it. This may be a good alternative on those days," I reply as I look at the bottle. I check the ingredients to be sure it's gluten- and dairy-free, which it is.

We chat a bit more about what I've been eating and the fiber supplement I've been using. She emphasizes that it really sounds to her like I'm doing everything I can to help the situation as best I can and that I have a good handle on my nutrition.

"I have some samples of this drink and I'm happy to leave those with you. And you can reach out to me anytime you need anything."

She hands me her card and gives Derek the bottles.

I'm glad it was only a ten-minute conversation because I am completely exhausted. I want to take a nap, but still have the ice in my hands and under my feet. Maria comes by to check on me and says I have about fifteen minutes left.

Soon, like a car alarm, the beep, beep, beep signals the end of Taxotere. I have to keep the ice on for another ten to fifteen minutes while Maria runs a flush through the IV and starts the Herceptin. I'm so ready to lie back and sleep.

Once the ice has been taken, I recline the chair, readjust the tiny, crinkly hospital-grade pillow, pull up my fluffy blanket, and try to settle in for some sleep.

My eyes close and I lie there, but sleep does not come. The chair moves in slow motion back to its upright position despite my attempts to keep it reclined, and it does this repeatedly. I resort to trying to sleep somewhat upright. The little pillow slides against the vinyl and I just cannot get comfortable.

"Ugh, this is so frustrating! I just want to sleep. I need to sleep," I say quietly but emphatically to Derek. A part of me doesn't want anyone else to hear me complaining.

I keep myself busy for the remainder of the treatment. We finish in about six and a half hours—and the entire time is without sleep. It seems like a cruel joke to not be able to sleep here. As if I must witness it all, with no space to disappear into dreamland.

At the same time, I know a lot of fatigue and sleep is in my near future. I thank the nurses as we leave and exit with a cheery, "See you in three weeks!"

Once home, I fall on the couch for some rest. When dinner rolls around, I stay downstairs with my family while they enjoy another meal sent by a friend. The smell begins to make me nauseated, so I excuse myself and head upstairs. It's about 7:30 p.m. and I treat myself to a footbath followed by distance Reiki from Rebecca again. As tired as I am, sleep continues to elude me. I see the clock turn to 1 a.m. and roll over, trying to ignore Derek's snoring.

At 7 a.m. I wake up with a slight headache, queasiness, and anxiousness, along with a rapid heartbeat.

It's that damn Decadron (steroid), and I still need to take another this morning.

I've realized if I can tolerate some light food, it actually keeps the nausea at bay a bit. The day becomes a cycle of trying to eat, trying to be present with my family, and trying to sleep. I'm trying my best and that's all I can ask for right now. That and a whole lot of grace, please!

* * *

Despite semi-loving my new 'do, hair inevitably continues to fall out. After a walk, I take off my baseball hat, only to find the inside covered in little hairs. I wake up in the morning with little hairs all over my pillowcase. I have quickly realized it is just as annoying, and gross, to shed short hairs as it was long ones, so I make the decision to shave it all off.

It is time to look like a fucking badass!

After seeing another breast cancer sister, Jennifer, do her head-shaving live on Facebook and feeling like I was there with her, I knew that was how I wanted to do it too. My community has been so incredibly supportive thus far and I want them all right by my side for this next step.

As mad as I have been about losing my hair and all the thoughts about looking like a cancer patient taking up residency in my mind, shaving my head no longer seems like as big of a deal at this point.

Perhaps it's due in part to having already conquered a daunting challenge last week, when those eight long ponytails were cut off, or maybe because I knew it was only a matter of time and have prepared myself. Whatever the reason, it seems like more of a formality at this point. It is the next step and it is time.

On Friday, April 9, I post on Facebook:

Derek will be shaving my head LIVE here on FB at 4 p.m. EST TODAY! I'm doing this live, so I can feel all your tremendous love and support through technology. Hope you'll join us and help me through this next step of #embracingcancer.

At 4 p.m. we start the live video. In our bathroom, I sit on the shower stool that has supported me in the shower post-surgery, with a ratty blue towel wrapped around my shoulders, facing our vanity mirror. I am blown away by the number of people I can see are watching this video.

"You ready?" Derek asks, holding the razor in his hand. Jacob stands behind him, a nervous smile on his face.

I glance at the mirror in front of me and then at my phone screen and know I am surrounded, in person and virtually, by the most amazing support system.

"Let's do this!" I confidently reply. I don't know where the bold optimism comes from and can only hope it stays with me.

Derek takes the razor to my head and I inhale, exhale, and find myself naturally smiling, no forcing it.

"Whoa, that's a lot of hair!" I say, as my hair falls to the floor.

"It's so dark," Derek comments over the buzz of the razor.

With the sides shaved, several people comment on the live video that we should leave the mohawk. Fun idea, if the hair in the middle of the crown of my head hadn't already fallen out.

"Can I shave some?" Jacob quietly asks.

I am taken aback and my heart swells at the same time.

Perhaps it's not as scary for the boys as I thought it might be.

He isn't quite sure how to use the razor, so Derek helps him. He successfully shaves a little bit before quickly passing the razor back to Derek.

Every now and then I glance up, catch my reflection in the mirror or the video, and feel so empowered.

I'm a total fucking badass!

Zachary comes in right as Derek finishes. Coincidentally, he shaved his head recently, not knowing this would be happening.

"Look, we match, Z," I say as I pull him next to me, wrapping him in a hug and planting a big kiss on his cheek.

I am uplifted by everyone who is on the Facebook live video. Their comments throughout this experience make me feel like everyone is right here with me, showering me with love through this next step.

"Thank you all for sharing in this moment with me! Your love carries me through!" I say as we end the video.

I had put so much energy into worrying about what it would be like to "look like a cancer patient" and had such fear around it. Now, as I stand up and shed the towel, I rub my bald head with a boldness I never could've imagined.

* * *

Only two days later, the tide of emotions shift, when my entire body is in pain and I can't do anything other than sleep. I sign on to RAW, my morning journaling community, hopeful it will lift my spirits. Even if I don't have the energy to write, the presence and energy of my RAW sisters will lift me up. Alisha's soothing voice brings the peace I need right now, and it grounds me deeply. When it is time for us to journal, the words come easily.

April 11, 2021
Mad.
So fucking mad.
Tired.
The pain.
Don't want to be positive, brave, or strong...
Want to be normal, out doing what I should be doing.
Can't cry because it hurts.
Everything hurts.
Crumbling inside and don't know how to let it out.
Don't even know what I'm feeling.

When we come back together to reflect, I share what I've written with my trusted RAW sisters.

I then add, "Everyone tells me how brave and strong I am and I know it is with the best intentions. Yet, anger still brews inside of me. I am not mad at the people. I am mad at cancer. I don't want to have cancer. I don't want this to be the reason I have to be brave and strong. I don't want any of this."

I look at each of their faces and can feel their love and support. They don't try to fix any of it for me. They sit in the shit with me, holding space for me. I appreciate every second.

After we close, I am completely worn out. The crying and emotional release is healthy and exhausting. Cancer is a see-saw of emotions.

Just days ago I was a badass, feeling the strength to conquer anything. Today I am mad and grieving the loss of:

- the life I had, my "normal" life
- my healthy body
- my ability to be the mom I want to be and to care for my kids
- control—over so many things

So quickly again, it feels like cancer has taken the wheel in my life, and I fucking hate it. I keep so much of this anger to myself and my journal, yet I know it is not healthy to only do these things. I must find ways to safely get these feelings out of me. I can't only rely on my time in RAW. My therapist suggests ways to let these feelings out: scream in a car by myself, scream into a pillow, or go to one of those rage rooms where

I could break shit. I just can't, or perhaps won't allow myself, to release any of these emotions.

If I express anger or any negative emotions, aren't I losing who everyone thinks I am, who I have come to expect of myself? Am I no longer "Amy" but rather "Amy with cancer"? Am I allowing cancer to define me?

In moments of clarity, I know this is shame creeping in and not my truth. The brain can be an incredible gift and a nightmare. When I feel called to, I reveal little bits of my reality through my blog and social media posts, but I don't fully release the rage. It's like I am a pressure cooker and I only open the valve a tiny bit. I won't dare pop the top off and let all the steam out. It just isn't something I can do right now. It feels too shameful.

As I approach my third round of chemo, I remind myself that I cannot control what is happening to me but I can control how I respond to all of it.

April 26 Journal Entry:

What I know to be solid and true:
My husband loves me and would do anything for me;
I can only control what I can control;
I am doing the best I can and what is true to me in fighting cancer;
I am surrounded by positive, healing energy and people who love me;
I am learning and growing spiritually every day;
I am enough, as I am, in any given moment;
Nature, and the beach specifically, heal me;
Our home is filled with love.

CHEMO ON MY BIRTHDAY? (4/26/21)

With two days until my third round of chemo, I head to Dr. Ramirez's office for blood work, just as I have for the previous two rounds.

When Melissa, the nurse practitioner, checks in, I can tell something is up.

"Your platelet levels are 94, which is low. We want them to be at least 142. I spoke with Dr. Ramirez and, with levels that low, she's just not comfortable treating you this week. We're going to delay one week to May fifth and give your body time to get the platelet levels up," she explains.

With tears welling up, I adamantly respond, "No! May fifth is my birthday." I know it doesn't matter, yet I still want her to know I'm upset about this.

"I know. It's not the ideal situation," she says with compassion. Melissa is always so kind to me.

I head to the front desk and reschedule the appointment. As I walk back to my car, I feel anger rising in my belly. I want to scream. I want to cry. I am fuming on the inside.

Chemo on my fucking birthday?

I get in my car and immediately call my sister. She doesn't answer, so I take a deep breath and call my parents. My dad answers and I start crying as soon as I hear his voice, the anger coursing through my veins.

"Honey! What's wrong?" he says with concern in his voice.

"Dad. I have to have chemo on my fucking birthday. This sucks. I fucking hate cancer so much. It's like I have no control over any of this and I can't stand it. You know how much I love celebrating my birthday, and now I have to spend it sitting in an infusion chair, hooked up to drips of medicine, getting chemo all day. It sucks."

"Slow down and tell me more. Why can't you have chemo this week?"

I explain it all to him, with my focus remaining on my birthday while his is more on my low blood counts.

With panic in his voice, he continues, "I understand why you don't want to be in that chair on your birthday. And more importantly I'm wondering what you can do to raise your platelets. Is there anything you can do to help?"

Here's my dad, knowing his daughter is unable to receive the medicine that's meant to help her.

I lean into his point of view and am able to understand the frightfulness of the situation. We continue to talk through it and by the time we reach the end of our chat, I am at least able to see a positive side to the situation at hand. The past two rounds I didn't feel sick on chemo day, so at least I shouldn't be feeling too bad on my birthday! I joke that I'll wear a birthday sash and a tiara to chemo and maybe even bring some balloons and tie them to my chair.

Many of the emotions that I categorize in my optimist's mind as "negative" have begun creeping in more and more. As the scales begin to tip, "fuck cancer" is starting to be louder than "embrace cancer." While it's louder in my mind, I still have a hard time allowing myself to feel these feelings and don't quite know how to express them. It feels like a sign of weakness to do so. If I declare myself a serial optimist, how could I feel these so-called "negative" emotions?

They are feelings I have shoved down for as long as I can remember.

As the happy, sunny, smiling one, I couldn't express anger, fear, rage, or envy, right?

Perhaps everyone else was waiting for it? "When is she going to drop the rose-colored glasses?"

I truly never expected this. Having a positive mind-set is my way and this all feels way too heavy. It makes me question whether being a serial optimist has all been worth it. Right now, I don't want to be a serial optimist.

A VIRUS AND A BIRTHDAY SURPRISE (4/27/21–5/5/21)

I have been feeling quite anxious and worried about how the delay in treatment might affect the overall efficacy of the chemotherapy.

Will the chemo still work?
What if my body is rejecting the medicine?
What if I can't get chemo next time?

Before this past week, I hadn't even considered there might be a delay in treatment. I mean, I knew this sometimes happened, but the fact of it happening to me hadn't run through my mind.

In sharing the news and my feelings with Leigh about the delay, we agree it would be a good idea to get away for a few days and clear my head. We really like to be together, and when cancer first entered the picture, we knew it would be important to escape the realities of life at times. We decide to head to St. Michaels, Maryland, which is just a couple of hours from home.

I always enjoy our car rides and the time it gives us to catch up without our everyday distractions. We tend to get very into our conversations, so much so that one time, years ago, we completely missed a major turn in our route and didn't realize it for almost an hour. Despite being tired, I want this car trip to be like those of the past, so we fill it with great chats. Thankfully, we don't miss any turns.

Once we arrive, we check in at our hotel and decide to enjoy some pool time. Since it's been three weeks since my last chemo, I feel quite good, outside of some exhaustion. For the next two days we will relax, take walks, shop, and have many of our epic, wonderful sister chats. Thankfully, I have an appetite, which means we're able to indulge in good food, like a delicious caprese salad, pasta primavera, and even some wine. A friend of mine who beat breast cancer years ago created the term "ABC meetings—Anything But Cancer!" for those times when she wanted to spend time together focusing on anything but cancer. This is an ABC trip!

The two days fly by. This was just what my soul needed. Of course, it hasn't been a cure-all, and I am still feeling anxious about all the uncertainties. As we drive home on Friday, April 30, I feel more ready to face my cancer again and have come to terms with spending my birthday, May 5, in the chemo chair.

On Saturday, May 1, I wake up around 4 a.m. with horrendous abdominal cramping. I have been unable to sleep and keep running from bed to the bathroom, feeling as though I am going to be sick. It's 8:45 a.m. and my stomach pain has given way to diarrhea. By 9:15 a.m. I've added dry heaving and throwing up to this list. By 11:15 a.m. I have become incredibly weak and my entire body is shaking.

"Derek, I think we need to call the doctor or I need to go to the ER. This can't be good for me."

He calls Dr. Ramirez's office and speaks to the on-call oncologist. The doctor tells us to go to the ER, as the vomiting and diarrhea have not let up at all. Derek arranges for Zachary to go to our neighbor's house and the older boys stay home.

As we enter the ER, I am clenching a big plastic bowl in my hands and holding it up to my mouth. While checking in, I vomit into the bowl. The woman checking us in says she'll take the bowl and hands me a plastic, blue hospital vomit bag, just like the ones I had after surgery and during chemo. I go to the bathroom a few times, as I think I'm going to vomit or have diarrhea, but neither happen. I'm taken back to a bed and checked in by the nurse. After answering an initial round of questions, including allergies and medications I'm taking, they give me an IV of fluids and medicine to hopefully stop the cramping, vomiting, and diarrhea. Over the course of the next six hours at the ER, drugs are administered, a lot of blood is drawn, a COVID test is given, and I have a CT scan of my abdomen and pelvis.

"Derek, there's no sense in waiting here. Why don't you go home and check on the boys and come back?" I suggest since it's now nearly dinnertime.

We are then told that Derek won't be allowed to come back into the ER if he leaves, due to COVID. He will need to meet me in the lobby once I'm discharged.

"I think you should go. I'm probably fine, especially since the medicine has done its job. It's just a matter of time and getting results back before I'll be discharged."

He agrees and heads home. After a couple more hours, all tests come back normal, and it has been determined I likely have a very bad stomach virus. I am discharged with instructions to call Dr. Ramirez on Monday and to come back if any symptoms return. I have to be very careful of dehydration and low blood count levels.

I rest a lot and take it easy the rest of Saturday night and Sunday. First thing Monday morning I call Dr. Ramirez. Due to my virus and low white blood cell counts, she does not feel comfortable administering chemo on May 5.

I've gotten my wish of no chemo on my birthday. Instead, I am weak and recovering from this awful virus that has attacked my body. We will reevaluate my blood counts next Monday, with hopes that all will be well and we can resume treatment on May 12.

Fearful thoughts around these delays in treatment occupy my mind again. This time even stronger, as the delays have become longer.

As I lie in bed on my forty-fourth birthday, exhausted and weak, my sister FaceTimes me. Knowing she likely wants to wish me a happy birthday and it would bring a smile to my face, I answer the call. We've only been talking for a minute or two when my bedroom door opens. I assume it's Derek, so I lift my head to look in that direction.

"What? What? Seriously?" I scream.

To my surprise and delight, my mom and dad are standing there. In my room! I am beyond shocked and begin crying tears of joy as they walk over to my bed. I cry and hug them tighter than I may have ever done before.

"Happy birthday!" they both say.

I can't stop smiling and shaking my head in complete disbelief that they are here.

They tell me they'll be staying for the weekend and then they'll be back again for chemo on the twelfth. Derek, Leigh, and my parents had been plotting this sweet surprise for me. While I still don't feel well, this provides some much-needed uplifting moments for me. Perhaps for all of us.

SPIRIT
(5/8/21–5/19/21)

I notice Jen's eyes get a little watery as she says, "That you'll lose your spirit. Your Amy spirit."

Jen and I have known each other for about ten years. We met through business and she has become a very close friend of mine. We can sit down for coffee and next thing we know it's been three hours of talking, laughing, and sometimes crying. It's usually me crying, as Jen isn't as much of a crier as I am.

She reached out to see if I'd like to get together during this lull in chemo. I appreciate her thoughtfulness, and since I am feeling better, I take her up on her invitation.

It is a beautiful day, and we decide to sit outside at one of our favorite cafés. Due to both the nice weather and COVID, a lot of other people are sitting outside as well. We chat for a couple of hours about my treatments, work, kids, and marriage—all the things we always talk about.

She pauses, looks me straight in the eyes, and asks, "What is your biggest fear right now?"

Whew! That's a big question and I find myself unable to answer. I don't want to think about fear, so I tell her I don't really know.

"Do you want to know mine?" she leans in and asks.

Oh shit. Here we go. She's going to talk about me dying.

Jen lost another friend to breast cancer only a few years ago and I know it really hit her hard.

I can't go there right now. Not in front of all these people. I'm in survival mode.

I am curious to know what her fear is, though. Maybe it doesn't have to do with death?

"Sure," I sheepishly reply.

And that's when she says it, her eyes filled with tears, "That you'll lose your spirit. Your Amy spirit."

I let out a deep breath as her words fill me with both relief and overwhelm. Then I ask her to please say more.

"What I love so much about you, Amy, is your optimism, your ability to listen to others, and how you are lifting people up even through your own challenges. You are at peace with yourself, who you are, and what you're here for. You are teaching people tools to find peace within themselves, through your own stories coupled with their own experiences. It's truly beautiful and it's what makes you you."

Here I thought she was worried about me dying, and she was just wanting me to keep my spirit. Wow!

"Oh, Jen! I'll never lose that. Never! It's who I am and I so appreciate you seeing that within me."

As they leave my mouth, I truly believe these words. I feel solid in who I am and how I show up in the world. I am overwhelmed at the recognition Jen has shown me today, in how she sees this quality in me too.

We finish our lattes and wrap up our conversation with hugs. I drive home with a full belly and an even fuller heart. I smile with gratitude for the strong bonds of friendship I have to carry me through life, especially in the most challenging of times.

On May 10, I return for my pre-chemo blood work. My leg bounces with nerves as I wait in the exam room. What will Dr. Ramirez come in and tell me?

Think positive thoughts, Amy.

As soon as she walks in, I know the answer from the look of disappointment on her face. The counts are still too low to have treatment. At this point, I am incredibly worried, as my every three weeks for chemo has now turned into five weeks.

"Your white blood cell count is low, at only 3.13, and your neutrophils are very low, only around 300. Neutrophils are the most abundant type of white blood cells. They kill off bacteria and help your body do things like fight infections and heal wounds. It's important that they're high enough to do their job because, as you know, chemo unfortunately also kills so many healthy cells in the process of killing cancer cells. A count of 1,000 is the lowest limit I'd feel safe administering Taxotere and Carboplatin. I spoke with the clinical pharmacist and he agrees that, given these numbers, we just can't move ahead with this treatment as it stands."

She notices me tearing up and quickly interjects, "But, there are other options."

I nod and say okay to let her know I'm listening.

"To start, while I can't give you TC tomorrow, I don't want to bail completely, so I'd like to go ahead with your Herceptin and Perjeta, as those shouldn't affect your counts at all."

I reach over for my notebook and pen and start writing furiously. I know my parents will have questions and Derek isn't here as a second set of ears.

WBC 3.13 low.
Neutro-something? 300 needs to be at least 1,000—needed to fight infections.
No TC tomorrow—Yes HP.

"We're going to try what I do for my little old lady patients whose bodies can't tolerate large doses of chemotherapy. Rather than every three weeks, you will now have Carboplatin and Taxol every week, but at a lower dose. Every three weeks, you'll also receive the Herceptin and Perjeta, as scheduled. Taxol is similar to Taxotere so there shouldn't be any issues with that change. Fingers crossed."

Great, I'm getting the "little old lady" chemo.

I can't help but chuckle. Inside my stomach is in knots.

"How will these changes impact the efficacy of the chemo?" I ask with eyebrows raised.

Dr. Ramirez tells me this is still an effective treatment plan. She then takes the time to share some studies with me where this plan has proven successful, and she encourages me to look up studies online too.

"Okay, well I guess it's what we have to do. I just want to do what's going to get rid of the cancer and keep it out."

Before leaving, she explains to me that with this change I'll also need to have blood work done the day of chemo, rather than forty-eight hours prior. This is so the pharmacy can prescribe the medicine in real time, with the correct doses, based on that day's blood work. At first, this doesn't sound like any big deal. She then goes on to explain that the pharmacy is located in the main cancer center and I'll need to switch my treatments over to there.

Unfortunately her office, where I've been receiving chemo, doesn't have a pharmacy.

This is just too much. But it's what you have to do, Amy.

One final thing we talk about is a way to keep my counts high, which is by giving myself an injection of a medicine called Granix. She wants me to do this and have my blood drawn and checked on May 17 and then stop the injections to get a "clean" read at chemo on the nineteenth.

Chemo is scary enough, and now I am facing changes in meds and location, a new setup, and new nurses. It's a lot! Fear, worry, and anxiety course through my veins, the very place where my chemo meds should be flowing right now.

I acknowledge how lucky I am to have another option and I am also incredibly frustrated. Why does this have to be so fucking hard?

Some days cancer feels more like a spiritual journey than a physical one.

As I sink into a state of despair and fear, I can't help but reflect on my time with Jen and wonder how solid I truly am in my spirit. Throughout this cancer fuckery, I have recognized a loss of my sense of self and who I am.

Have I lost my spirit? If I am not optimistic and positive, am I even the same Amy? The one Jen loves so much?

MOVING FORWARD, OR IS IT BACKWARD?

(5/19/21)

I feel like I am starting all over. Here I am, on May 19, just six weeks shy of what would have been my chemo end date, starting a new plan. With a new end date of August 3, I go from having four treatments remaining to now having ten on the calendar.

My sister is here with me today and I'm so glad she can help me navigate all the newness. It should be a much shorter day since I will only be receiving Taxol and Carboplatin. That is, of course, only if my counts are high enough and Dr. Ramirez gives the go-ahead.

I stop at the lab on the first floor to have my blood drawn. Ryan, the tech, is very kind and compassionate. After he fills the three vials with my blood, he tells me to head on upstairs to the infusion center.

We navigate our way up one escalator to the main elevators and head up to the ninth floor. It is a silent elevator ride.

We locate the infusion center and see several other people waiting. I check in and get my wristband. I glance around the room and smile at an elderly man with an oxygen tank. The hospital-like smell and my internal fear bring about a wave of disgust inside my belly.

"You okay?" Leigh asks as we sit in the waiting room.

"I'm nervous. What if my counts aren't high enough again?"

"If that happens, we'll deal with it then. For now, try and relax," she calmly says in response.

My white blood cell count and neutrophils were both off-the-charts high just two days ago, thanks to the injections I've been doing.

"Amy Banocy," I hear from the far end of the waiting room.

I look at Leigh, raise my eyebrows, and we both walk that way.

The young nurse introduces herself as Megan and starts leading us down a long hallway. I'm overwhelmed by the size of this place, compared to Dr. Ramirez's office. There are rooms with sliding glass doors and there are also a bunch of recliners throughout the main space. People are getting treatment in these chairs with no privacy at all.

"Will I be in a room?" I ask Megan.

"Today you are, but there's no guarantee for other dates. It just depends on what time you come and how many other people are here at that time."

My stomach sinks.

I don't ever want to have chemo in this open area. I don't like this.

Once in the room, I sit in the infusion chair and Leigh takes a seat in the other chair. The chairs and equipment look newer here than at Dr. Ramirez's infusion suite.

Megan asks me the typical series of questions, takes my vitals, and types all my answers in the computer as I'm talking. She then turns to me and says, "Okay, I'm going to get your Carboplatin and we can get started," in an upbeat tone.

Wait, what? Did she already check my blood work? Do I have clearance from Dr. Ramirez?

I hesitate to question her but know I must advocate for myself.

"I don't know if my chart has been updated, but Dr. Ramirez is supposed to be called once my labs are in. Since my counts have been so low, she will decide then whether we're going ahead with treatment today."

She scrolls the computer and says, "Hmmm. I don't see that. Let me check what's going on."

She leaves and slides the glass door shut. Leigh and I exchange a "what the fuck?" look. I shrug my shoulders and shake my head in disbelief. How could they not know what's going on with a patient? What if I hadn't said anything?

Megan returns in about ten minutes. My blood work is back and she has spoken with Dr. Ramirez. My neutrophils are now hovering around 530, when they had just been over 2,000 two days ago.

I sigh in frustration.

"Because your body responded to the Granix, Dr. Ramirez knows your counts can in fact rebound. For some reason, they are plummeting without the Granix. She spoke with the clinical pharmacist here and wants to go ahead with treatment today, but at a partial dose. You'll then start the injections again in preparation for next week's treatment. Does that all make sense?"

It does, even though I don't like it. I don't want to receive only a partial dose. I don't want to give myself the injections again next week.

We move forward with the treatment for today. Carboplatin is relentless in its pursuit and brings me nausea once again. I manage it and am then able to rest. I recline in the blue vinyl chair, layer myself with blankets, and let my eyes close out the world.

When it is time, I slip on my white gloves and fuzzy socks in preparation for the chill of the ice packs. Leigh keeps asking if I'm okay. I know she means well. I'm going to say yes no matter what. There's nothing I can do about the situation, so

I just move through it as best I can. I'm exhausted but can't sleep because of the ice. It's all too uncomfortable.

When it's time to leave, I ask Megan if she can please note in my chart about needing to call Dr. Ramirez to give the all clear, so I don't run into the same issue next time. She assures me it will be in my chart before my next treatment.

In the days following treatment, I am quickly reminded of the fuckery cancer brings with it. Exhaustion, weakness, nausea, constipation, diarrhea, reflux, and flushed skin. I try to combat these with acupuncture, massage, and medical marijuana. While each provide short-term relief, nothing gives me the respite I seek.

By day five I feel physically better, but the monsters named "anxiety" and "depression" have arrived. After acupuncture, I sit alone in my car and cry. I want to be done with this shit and know what a long road still lies ahead. To add insult to injury, Dr. Ramirez has decided to move back my next treatment a few days, with the hope that extra injections will help keep my counts high.

Leigh is with me again and we keep our fingers crossed as we wait for results of my blood work. After running through the intake questions, it becomes apparent my chart has not been updated when my nurse, Julie, says she will be back with premeds.

It is the same thing all over again and I am too damn tired for this shit today. Leigh senses it and speaks up on my behalf. Julie leaves to call Dr. Ramirez.

My sweaty back sticks to the vinyl chair as I continuously hit refresh on my patient portal app. I know by now that I'll see the results before Julie will come in and tell me.

"Shit, Leigh! They're low again," I say as tears fall from my eyes. "I can't take this shit."

Before she can respond, Julie has returned.

"Dr. Ramirez wants to go ahead with Taxol today, at a reduced dose. She doesn't feel comfortable administering Carboplatin with how low your numbers are. She also wants you to do the Granix injections for four nights, starting tonight," she relays with kindness in her voice.

The next day brings a welcomed break in the storm. Our application to adopt a rescue dog has been approved. We are thrilled Tess will join our family in a few weeks.

I have a phone appointment with Dr. Ramirez today and am anxious to discuss what the hell is going on with my body. The initial plan was to do the injections for only a week or so, but my body just isn't reacting as expected. My counts spike with the injections and then plummet again once the medication is out of my system.

"I haven't seen this before, and I'm wondering if there might be some underlying issue, rather than just the virus, affecting your counts. I want you to meet with an oncology hematologist, so we can get a better idea of what is happening," she tells me. It sounds like she is at somewhat of a loss here.

Now I am even more frightened at the thought that something else could be going on.

Dr. Crane, the hematologist, is incredibly thorough and understands all my expressed fears and concerns. She believes this is all still from the virus I had, and it would seem incredibly unlikely there would be any cancer in my blood causing these low numbers.

"Your body is responding to the injections and your blood work isn't showing a lot of immature blast cells, which would be a sign something else may be going on. We definitely want to be certain that's not the case, so I'm going to order a lot of lab work as well as a bone marrow biopsy."

A bone marrow biopsy? What in the actual fuck? Do I have leukemia? Is this a blood disorder?

She sends me to have blood drawn that day, but I won't be able to have the biopsy for another three weeks. During this time, so many thoughts run through my head and I have trouble calming my mind. I try to use meditation and my spiritual practices to keep me centered, but it is a challenge.

The bone marrow biopsy is a harrowing experience. Thankfully the results are normal. I breathe a sigh of relief and in the next breath wonder about my blood counts.

Both Dr. Crane and Dr. Ramirez agree the low count may be from the virus and that my body is just taking longer than average to recover. So, the goal has become simply getting through and doing what I need to do to finish chemo. This now means giving myself injections every week, for three to four days leading up to my chemo treatment in order to boost my counts.

This sucks, mentally and physically.

After weeks of this, I am filled with frustration and question whether chemo is even the right path anymore. I tell Dr. Ramirez, "I feel like I'm tricking my body into thinking it's strong enough, just to put these drugs in it, to maybe kill the cancer cells."

"I don't disagree with you, Amy. That is what you're doing, and if you want to get through chemo, it's what you need to continue doing," she says with compassion in her voice.

I know I want to finish the treatments and give myself the best chance at killing cancer as well as reducing my chances of recurrence.

I receive such wonderful support during this exhausting and trying time. I feel lucky for every meal delivery, card, and check-in and for those who sit with me during chemo. I am also deeply saddened that I have not heard from some people I thought would show up for me and from some who even told me they would. I try not to focus on it, but it stings.

SUPPORT!

My friend Courtney has driven up from Savannah, Georgia, to spend a couple of days with me and I absolutely cannot wait to be together. She's whisking me away to a hotel in Washington, DC, that has a rooftop pool and is surrounded by delicious restaurants. Since I had chemo yesterday, I am crossing my fingers I feel well enough to enjoy our time together. My bag is packed and I am anxiously awaiting her arrival at my house.

"She's here! She's here!" I shout out with excitement when I see her van pull up in the driveway.

I want to run down the steps and hug her, and at the same time I'm too tired, knowing I'll have to come back up and get my stuff. So, I meet her at my front door and grab her into a bear hug.

"Oh, Amy! I am so happy to be here with you. It's hard being so far away from you through all this," she says as we hug.

I know both of us need this visit and time together. Courtney picks up my bag, and we get in her van and head into DC. It's about a twenty-minute ride and I feel somewhat dizzy and nauseated. I take my antinausea med and try to close my eyes.

Damn it. I just want to feel good and enjoy this time together!

We make it to the hotel, which is absolutely gorgeous! Once in the room, Courtney enthusiastically says, "Let's have a toast, my friend. I know you can't have the real stuff so I got you this hydration drink. It'll look just like champagne in your glass."

She fills a glass for me, pops open the champagne for her, and fills her glass.

"To friendship and health and you kicking cancer's ass!" she says.

We clink glasses and each take a sip. Mine definitely doesn't taste like champagne but I appreciate her thoughtfulness. We snap a couple selfies and then relax, catch up, and head to bed with a movie on in the background.

Today is a beautiful, sunny day. We walk to a nearby café for breakfast. It has outdoor seating, which is important because of the COVID-19 precautions and my immune system being compromised due to chemotherapy.

It is so lovely to sit outside and enjoy our breakfast and some good conversation.

Shit! Is that another fucking nosebleed I feel? Not again. Not here.

I reach for a napkin, thinking it's probably just little trickle since I haven't had a nosebleed in a while. The napkin quickly becomes soaked through and I now know it is a massive nosebleed. I grab the few remaining napkins on the table and Courtney runs inside the café to get more napkins and to ask for some ice.

This is so embarrassing.

I just want to hide when I notice a woman looking at me. No, not looking, staring. You know when you see something and your eyes become fixated on it, but you know you should look away. That's how she looks. Like she knows she shouldn't stare but just can't help herself.

Is she staring at me because I am this bald woman with a bloody nose, so she assumes cancer and feels bad for me? Or is she looking at me thinking how gross this is and how I should leave? Or does she feel bad for me and wish she could help? Gosh, I really wish she'd stop looking at me. This is so fucking embarrassing. Maybe we should leave.

Thankfully Courtney is back with a bag of ice and more napkins.

"Is there anything else I can do to help?" she asks with so much care in her voice.

I hold the makeshift tissues to my nostrils and the bag of ice awkwardly positioned on the bridge of my nose.

I tell her, "No. You've been so helpful. I'm so embarrassed and I fucking hate this, Court. I can't even get away from cancer for a day."

I can see the compassion in her eyes as she reassures me there is absolutely nothing to be ashamed of.

I look over at where the woman is sitting, and she is no longer staring at me. A switch flips and I know I have gone from embarrassment to pure anger.

I am so mad at cancer for ruining what is supposed to be a nice breakfast with my friend who's come all this way to visit me. Why couldn't I just have this moment, like it would've been before cancer invaded my body?

Because cancer is a beast that gives constant reminders of its presence.

Hey, cancer, you've made your place in my body, but you don't have to continue to remind me every time I try to do something fun.

We enjoy the rest of the day, including time at the rooftop pool and a nap for me while Courtney went to the gym. I am thankful that nausea is the only discomfort I feel, as it's one I'm used to at this point and know how to manage with medication and other treatments.

As we drive back to my house, I am filled with gratitude for Courtney and our time together, especially knowing another chemo is right around the corner. Having chemo every week makes it seem like I am always there. The days in between treatments go by too quickly. The first few bring nausea and fatigue, and the next few bring preparation for the following treatment. I am in a routine now, even administering the injections myself. It has all become the norm, which brings a layer of resentment and sorrow for what my life has become.

This week's chemo will be different. Well, not the treatment itself but the days afterward. For eighteen years my family and extended family have taken a beach trip to the Outer Banks together. I look forward to it all year. Not only because the beach is my happy place and my home but also because I love the time together. When I was switched to weekly chemo, one of my first worries was whether I'd be able to make it to the annual trip. Now that I know better how the chemo affects me, I told my mom, "I'd rather feel sick and be steps from the beach than feel sick and be home while you're all there."

The plan is for my sister and her husband to drive my boys down with their family on Sunday. Derek and I will stay back and head to the beach either after chemo Wednesday or on Thursday morning, depending on how I am feeling. Chemo is at 9 a.m. Wednesday, so I am really hopeful we will go that afternoon or evening. I'm pissed I have to miss any time there and want as much time as I can get.

Derek and I have our bags packed and at the front door when we head to chemo. First stop, as always, is the lab for blood work. With that finished, we take the elevator up to the infusion center. Once settled in my room, the nurse asks me the typical slew of questions and I'm hardly bothered by any of it. All I am focused on is getting through chemo and to the beach.

I'm frustrated because once again my information has not been updated in my chart. I go through the same back and forth with the nurses, who aren't aware they need to contact Dr. Ramirez. Once that's taken care of, the rest of the treatment goes well.

Afterward, we rush home, grab our bags, lock up the house, and are on our way. I sleep the majority of the drive, and when I do wake up it's only to take nausea medicine. We arrive at the beach house around 9 p.m.

Everyone is so excited to see us. Shouts of, "You made it!" come from various family. Zachary runs up and gives me a huge hug. Andrew and Jacob follow suit. I'm exhausted and know I need to go to sleep. As I say goodnight to everyone and head downstairs, I say a silent prayer that I will be well enough to go to the beach tomorrow. Even if only in the late afternoon, when it tends to cool off a bit.

I make it to the beach Thursday as well as each day thereafter. I am able to watch Jacob take surfing lessons, which he loves. I don't spend as much time on the beach as usual and I certainly don't sit in the sun as much. I bring nausea meds in my cooler and take them throughout the day. I am bald and it is obvious, even under my baseball cap. I don't make it to family dinner every night nor am I able to enjoy wine with the adults as I usually would. Despite all this, it is still better than missing this trip altogether.

As we prepare to leave on Sunday, my mom hugs me and says, "When I saw you walk down to that ocean, I was so joyful and happy. It was a very, very special time. And even though you were very tired all week, I am so glad you were well enough to be with us because it wasn't a definite that you'd come."

This annual family vacation means the world to me, and it was such a sweet spot in my cancer fuckery. And now it begins again, the injections and premeds, as I prepare for chemo on Wednesday. This is my life.

"I will not let cancer define me!"

I can remember the exact moment I declared these words to my sister. We were spending a few days together at the beach at the end of January 2021, just a couple of weeks prior to my bilateral mastectomy surgery. It was quite chilly but we wanted to get out for a walk, so we bundled up and made our way to the boardwalk.

As we were nearing the end of our walk Leigh said, "So, we haven't talked much about your surgery while we've been away. How are you feeling about everything? Anything you want to talk about?"

"No. I feel fine about it. It's gonna be fine. I'm gonna be fine. I'll have the surgery and that'll be it with cancer for me. I will not let cancer define me!"

I was feeling so strong and confident when I said that. I felt deep in my bones that I did not want to become someone who talked about breast cancer all the time or had lots of stuff with pink ribbons on it. I have never been a fan of the pink ribbon, even before my own diagnosis. A friend who had battled breast cancer years before once talked about how pink is a pretty color and there is absolutely nothing pretty about cancer. That has always stuck with me.

On that chilly January day, as we walked along the boardwalk, I truly thought and felt I'd have the bilateral mastectomy, they'd take my boobs, and cancer would be out of my body and out of my life. That's how the doctors had made it seem and so I was going with it.

Little did I know at that time that losing my breasts would only be the beginning of my cancer marathon, and breast cancer would indeed become a large part of my identity.

As time and my treatments have progressed, cancer seems to have become the topic of nearly every conversation I have with people.

"When's your next treatment?"

"When's your next appointment?"

"What'd the doctor say?"

I find myself answering questions like these over and over again. Some days it feels like I don't talk about anything other than cancer. It has become the central point of my conversations. In my heart I know people ask questions like these out of genuine care and concern, and for that I am grateful. At the same time, answering the same questions repeatedly is incredibly draining, no matter the situation, and it's even more challenging in the midst of cancer. The lack of "normal" or "noncancer" conversations make me feel like a shadow of myself.

While it makes me irate, I ironically find myself falling into the same trap. I no longer focus conversations on past Amy either. I don't talk about my work or what book I'm reading. Most of the time it's cancer, cancer, cancer.

When I have enough energy to post on social media, it is usually an update on something related to cancer: how I am feeling, how my treatments are going, or what the next steps will be. I rarely post pictures of my family or share about other parts of my life as I once did on these platforms.

I visit Facebook groups for women with breast cancer. I participate in the conversations there and ask my own questions too.

While I hate cancer being the central focus, I also perpetuate it. My life is ruled more and more by cancer, chemo, depression, anxiety, future radiation treatments, and doctor appointments.

Cancer *is* defining me! I was wrong! I don't like to be wrong, especially about big things in life. (Yes, I know it's something I have to work on—wink, wink!)

I am a failure. I said I wouldn't let this disease define me. I'm not living up to my promise to myself. More than it being about failure, I am deeply ashamed because this all feels like cancer has, in some way, won a piece of me.

I've kept this feeling to myself for a while, probably out of shame, which was never a good idea.

Shame grows inside every part of me. Shame feels lonely. Shame feels revolting. Shame feels like a dark cloud hanging over me.

I am meeting Leigh for coffee this morning and have worked up the courage to share my feelings. She always has a way of making me feel significantly more whole. I'm extremely lucky to have her in my corner, especially during all this cancer fuckery.

We meet at one of our favorite spots, a coffee shop at Lake Anne Plaza, located in the area where we grew up. It holds special meaning for both of us.

In the midst of conversation about how I feel, I sniffle and wipe my index finger across the base of my eyes.

"I've always been a positive person. Everyone knows me as a positive person. So if I'm feeling all this anger and rage, then I'm not who I say I am. I'm failing at being myself and cancer is winning," I manage to choke out.

She reaches across the table, grabs my hand in hers, and looks right into my tearful eyes.

"Oh, Amy. You're not failing. You are being a genuine, honest person. You are not letting cancer define you. You are going to do big things because of this experience. I don't know what it'll be but I know you, and I know you'll do something impactful. You have to feel these feelings. It's all part of the process," she says with gentle compassion.

I am grateful to be surrounded by people who love me and who remind me of the bright light I am.

My mom is also one of my cheerleaders and I'm excited she is in town to sit with me during chemo this week. We spend the day before at a beautiful resort in town. We relax, sit at the pool, nap, read, and spend quality time together. At night I have to give myself the Granix injection and reality hits again.

I have a love-hate relationship with chemo. I hold faith it is supporting me in killing the cancer, so I push through the fuckery it causes my body, and hold tight and close the days, hours, and minutes when I do feel good and have energy to enjoy the simple things.

When we arrive at the cancer center, my mom's anxiety is palpable. She does not mean to put her anxiety on me, but her face wears it and it is undeniable. Once in the room, she floods my nurse with questions. I try to remember her daughter has cancer and is sitting in the chair across from her about to get poisoned by chemotherapy. I try to appreciate her concern, rather than be frustrated by it.

She can't believe it when I have to tell the nurse, yet again, about calling Dr. Ramirez. At this point I expect it and it still pisses me off. Here I am, a cancer patient, under extreme duress and exhaustion, and I have to repeat this shit every week. There is absolutely no reason why this can't be added to my chart.

Next week is my last chemo treatment and the last time I'll have to repeat this info. For today, I enjoy my mom's company and her endless love.

When we get home she tells me, "That was gut-wrenching. To see those drugs go into you and only hope that it kills everything and does its job. You are my daughter, my light."

LAST TC CHEMO (8/3/21)

It has been a long road and I have finally reached my last day of "the tough chemo drugs" Taxol and Carboplatin. I know about the ritual of ringing a bell when one finishes chemo, and in recent weeks I've spent a lot of time thinking about how I will honor this ending and whether it will include ringing the bell.

I am conflicted because, while I'll be finished with these meds—and yes, they are known to be tougher on the body than Herceptin and Perjeta—the fact remains that I have a long way to go with my treatments. Technically HP is immunotherapy, not chemotherapy, but I will not feel I am finished with treatment today. I will still have my port; I will still be poked, prodded, and hooked up to receive IV drugs. Yes, the side effects should be less with HP. Yes, each treatment will be half as long. Yes, I'll be going every three weeks rather than every week. I recognize all these as big wins. I also recognize something just doesn't feel right to me in calling my treatment "finished."

Traditionally, many people ring the bell when they finish chemo, as a way of celebrating that moment, and that's awesome if it feels right to them. I haven't quite decided what I'll do at the end of treatment today, but I do know something about ringing that bell just isn't vibing with me. At this time, I feel ringing the bell would be more for other people than for me.

I was chatting with one of the oncology therapists who visited me during chemo last week and I had a big aha moment.

"Many of my patients feel that much of society believes, feels, or associates the end of chemo with the end of cancer. For you, and many others, chemo is not the end at all," she shared with me.

Yes! That's it!

I realized then that part of me doesn't want to make a big public deal about finishing chemo because, while it is a huge step, it is not the end of this cancer journey. Finishing chemo does not mean I am cancer free. It does not mean I am mentally, physically, or emotionally healed from any of this. It does not mean I'm finished. I still have at least one surgery, the anxiety-filled wait for pathology results, continued treatment for at least seven more months, radiation, and the possibility of other things I do not even know about yet.

That's how this cancer fuckery goes. Twists and turns. As we sat and talked, I realized that ringing the bell in recognition of finishing TC was perhaps telling society the opposite of how I really feel. Yes, I'll be elated when this part is finished and I hope I never have to do it again, but I'm still deep in this cancer shit and will be for quite some time.

While I won't be ringing the bell today, I do want to celebrate the win in some way. I still don't know exactly what that will look like, other than it will be in a way that feels good to me. I want to honor the completion of this step in the journey. If nothing else, I will walk out the door with my head held high, a smile on my face, and a feeling of victory!

All has been well today, as we plug right along through the different meds. Taxol has just finished filling my veins and has been turned off. I am in the final twenty minutes of icing my hands and feet. The nurse, Wendy, pulls on the protective gear, starts the Carboplatin, makes sure we're good to go, and leaves the room.

Derek and I are searching online for a family vacation we'd like to take before my next surgery. I abruptly look up at him with fear in my eyes and say, "I don't know why, but I don't feel very well."

Between March 17 and today I have successfully received Carboplatin ten times, in varying doses, so I think the pain in my back and slight wave of nausea I feel may be my imagination.

"Should I get the nurse?" he asks and I say, "No, it's probably fine."

Seconds later my answer changes and I tell him to get the nurse.

I am incredibly nauseated and my face is sweating. In an instant I am so hot, I feel like I need to strip naked in order to breathe.

Wendy and two other nurses rush in. They immediately stop the Carboplatin.

One nurse takes my vitals.

Another gathers info from Derek about what happened.

Another brings in an oxygen tank.

Someone takes the ice packs off my hands and feet.

Questions are asked between the nurses. So many people squeeze into this little room. So much noise.

"I'm gonna throw up. I need something to throw up in!"

One of the nurses hands me a blue, plastic hospital vomit bag and I immediately begin dry heaving.

I am burning up and use the little energy I have to ask for cold washcloths on my neck.

The dry heaving continues.

I hear the nurses ruling out any impact to my breathing. The oxygen tank stays in the room, though.

"Take deep breaths. You're having an allergic reaction to the Carboplatin, and it will go away," one nurse tells me as another now gently rubs my back.

I am slouched over, violently dry heaving as my sweaty body sticks to the vinyl seat.

What the hell was that? Did I just pee?

I wet myself. Yes, you read that correctly. I fucking wet myself.

I have no control over my body and hate this. I mean, sure, after delivering three babies, I've peed a little when I've sneezed before. But now? I suppose the contraction while dry heaving produced this result.

"I peed," comes out through the heaving and the tears. Embarrassment fills my every cell.

The nurse rubbing my back wipes my forehead and neck with the washcloth and kindly says, "It's okay. Don't even worry about it."

This can't be happening. Oh, my stomach!

"I need to get to the bathroom! I need to get to the bathroom!" I grunt as I feel diarrhea coming on.

I try to stand but I'm too weak and my stomach is cramping too much. A wheelchair is in front of me quickly, and two of the nurses help me move from the chair to the wheelchair.

As I'm wheeled down the hallway to the bathroom, I have terrible, loud dry heaving. I feel bad for other people around the infusion center who have to hear it all.

Today was supposed to be easy. Today was supposed to be some sort of celebration or acknowledgment.

I make it to the bathroom just in time. Thank goodness. I sit on the toilet and one of the nurses helps wiggle my pants off my body. The cramping is so intense I can barely tolerate it.

Please make it stop! Make it stop!

Nurses come in and out of the bathroom, talking about what medication they will give me—yes, I am still hooked up to IV—to help. Meanwhile, my amazing nurse Wendy continues to talk to me, helps me breathe, and alternates ice packs on my neck and cold washcloths on my face. The nurses' assistance is a team effort.

"Why is it taking so long to get the meds? I'm in so much pain!" I groan.

"We called in the order to the pharmacy and are just waiting for them to release the medicines. It should be any minute now, Amy. Just try to keep breathing. I know it hurts," Wendy says in a soothing voice. I look up and our eyes meet for just a moment. The connection is deep and I know she feels angry for me.

"Fuck! It hurts so bad!" I yell repeatedly. The nurses chuckle and tell me to scream as loud as I want. There is nothing pretty about this. I know it and they know it. Here I sit, disgusting and at probably my lowest human form, and they never once make me feel exposed or embarrassed.

I'm finally given: nausea medicine, a steroid to help with the cramping and Ativan for the overall reaction to this dose of Carboplatin. It takes a few minutes for the meds to kick in. The sweating decreases, the diarrhea and dry heaving subside, and I am able to return to my body.

Holy shit! That was bad!

I sit for a while as they monitor me to be sure this episode is actually finished. After some time, they give me clothes to change into. You know those huge, netted underwear you get after you've delivered a baby? Yup, *that* is what I wear. (Ladies, I'm here to tell you they've gotten better. Still not something I want to be wearing, but it is what it is.) I am just glad the pain has subsided.

I top the gorgeous mesh underwear with a pair of disposable scrubs—who knew such a thing existed?—and I am wheeled back to my room. Once back in the room, I glance up at the clock and see it is a quarter after. Initially this doesn't make sense because I recall looking at the clock shortly before all this happened, and it had been nearly a quarter after.

I know the episode was longer than a few minutes. I glance at the clock again, only to realize it had actually been an hour. An entire hour of pain, cramping, dry heaving, diarrhea, sweating, and cursing. An entire hour of Derek sitting in my infusion room without me, the nurses providing him with updates. An entire hour of amazing nurses taking care of me.

While all this has been going on, a nurse reached out to Dr. Ramirez regarding what to do next, since it's her call to make. Being my final dose, she sees no reason to even try administering Carboplatin again, even if at a slower dose.

Damn straight. That shit is never going in my body again!

I slump down in the blue vinyl chemo chair. I am exhausted, weak, and still in pain. I just want to go home and rest.

Wendy clears me to leave and the nurses ask if I want to be wheeled out to the car.

"No fucking way! The least I can do, on this final treatment, is *walk* out of here," I declare.

We wait until I feel well enough and can stand up on my own. When I have no dizziness or nausea, Derek and I very slowly walk out. My head may not be held high, as I am medicated, but I am not in that wheelchair, and I smile for this.

There really is no specific explanation for these reactions to Carboplatin on the bookends of my treatments. I choose to believe, for this one, my body was just *done* and this was its way of declaring loudly that it would not accept any more of these chemo meds. My body didn't just reject the meds with a little nausea, as it had during my first chemotherapy infusion in March. This time my body's rejection had me literally excreting the meds from every place it could.

Today, my body screamed, *"Nope! I am done here! No more of this chemo shit!"*

When we get home, I head straight to bed and quickly drift off to sleep.

That was terrifying! And it also totally sucks I didn't get to honor or celebrate my last chemo the way I had wanted as I was quite drugged up when I left there and definitely not in a celebratory state of mind. Rather than walking out with my head held high, jumping up and down, and high-fiving nurses, I could barely walk. Yet another bitch slap from cancer and a screaming reminder that this disease, these meds, this treatment, and my body, are making decisions without my consent.

A week later, I am back in the infusion suite, this time not to receive any chemotherapy. I arrive with gifts and hugs of gratitude for the nurses who showed me such incredible care during a very frightening episode.

"You never made me feel exposed. You were like sisters to me, keeping me calm and caring deeply for me the entire time," I share with them as tears well up in my eyes.

We share hugs, they tell me how brave I am, and I tell them how incredible they are. It is a lovefest of a different sort. As I walk out of the building, I have an extra pep in my step. The sun is shining, the sky is clear, and I realize I just honored my final TC.

I am filled with a deep sense of closure and relief.

SURGERY NUMBER TWO (9/14/21)

My amazing parents have come back to Virginia. They offer to stay with the boys while Derek and I enjoy a quiet couple of days away before my surgery. One of the things I love about where we live is the proximity to a variety of places. This time we decide to go to Harpers Ferry, West Virginia, which is only a couple of hours away. We enjoy meals without interruption, spend quality time together, and I even surprise myself by tackling a challenging hike.

When we reach the top and I find a flat rock to sit on, I gaze out at the mountains in the distance and the river below us. Silently, I reflect on all I have been through and all Derek has supported me through, and my heart is filled with gratitude. Derek has shown up for me in ways I will never be able to fully express my appreciation for. In a time of turmoil, he immediately rose to the occasion. I wonder what will be of our marriage when this cancer fuckery is over. Will we continue to cultivate the closeness we have in recent months, or will we return to the jagged rockiness we experienced before cancer invaded our lives?

I close my eyes, deeply inhale nature's gifts, and acknowledge the abundance of love in my life.

The day has finally come to get these horrible, uncomfortable, and unnatural tissue expanders out of my body. Due to the changes and delays in my chemo schedule, they've been in my body longer than expected and I am ready for their eviction. Dr. Mann, my plastic surgeon, will remove the tissue expanders and replace them with my implants. My breast surgeon, Dr. Bender, will clean out all the tissue in my underarm area surrounding where the two positive lymph nodes were found during my first surgery, as well as any other tissue she "deems suspicious." This tissue, which contains lymph nodes, will then be sent off to pathology.

An opposing sense of fear and relief are within me. The past two weeks have been absolutely gut-wrenching. One minute I think I'll be fine with implants and the next I'm scared shitless. What if I develop breast implant illness (BII)? What if my autoimmune symptoms heighten? BII may not be scientifically proven, but I've read a lot online and heard too many stories for me to not feel sick to my stomach at the thought of acquiring this condition. My options are either implants or flat closure, meaning no breasts. I've gone back and forth on these options too many times to count over these weeks.

Am I meant to be flat? Perhaps I am meant to be an advocate for flat? Am I only considering flat because it is the opposite of the big boobs I never loved? By having implants am I perpetuating a story that women need to have breasts to be whole? How will I feel when I am naked, either way?

I meditate, journal, speak with Dr. Mann, and trust my intuition. I've decided I'm not ready to be completely flat. I feel confident about my decision to move forward with implants yet anxious in my body. Last night was filled with moments of restlessness, my stomach and chest squeezed tight like a dishrag being wrung out.

I lie on my purple yoga mat and breathe deeply. I have shoved thoughts of this surgery to the back of my mind so I didn't have to face the reality of another surgery.

What if the pain is like the mastectomy? I can't handle that level of pain again.

Both Dr. Mann and Dr. Bender have conveyed that this surgery and the recovery are typically much easier on patients than the bilateral mastectomy with tissue expanders.

And then there's the lymph nodes and pathology; Dr. Bender and Dr. Ramirez are confident everything will come back clean. I'm not sure if they tell everyone this to keep our minds in a positive place or if they truly believe—between chemotherapy and taking my breasts—the cancer will be gone.

Either way, one thing is for sure. I am tired of doctors telling me their version of, "I really don't expect to find anything." I've heard it too many times now.

"Calcifications determined to be DCIS."

"It's caught early and surgery should be all it takes."

My MRI then shows widespread DCIS and I opt for bilateral mastectomy.

"We really don't expect to find anything in the lymph nodes."

Both lymph nodes taken are positive for cancer.

Post–bilateral mastectomy.

"The pain is normal and should decrease significantly within a week."

I close my eyes, inhale deeply, and promise to be gentle, kind, and loving to myself while I wait for these pathology results.

Last week was Rosh Hashanah, the Jewish New Year. In recent years I've separated myself more and more from organized religion and its institutions, and I've continued my own spiritual journey to discover what brings me peace and love.

For most of my life, I would sit in a synagogue service for hours on this holy day. This year I found new ways to honor this sacred day. My day consisted of movement, time spent in nature, reading, meditation, a discussion on the topic of "acceptance" with my RAW sisters, whom I connect with on a deep spiritual level, and, of course, a long nap.

I felt connected with spirit and more in tune and grounded than in past years. I thought about Rosh Hashanah and its meaning more than ever before. Thinking back to those synagogue services, I can recall stewing about how much longer I had to sit there and yucking it up with my friends as a way to make the best of it. Yes, even as an adult! Sure, there were moments that resonated with me, but on the whole, I was not really present to the meaning of the holy day. Removed from a typical way of worship, I found more connection to Rosh Hashanah and my Judaism than ever before.

As I head into this surgery, I think back to last week, when I wrote:

Rosh Hashanah means, to me, turning inward and thinking about how I can continue to grow and:

- *best trust myself and my intuition*
- *lead a life filled with value and purpose*
- *better serve my community and make a difference*

I am very confident the pathology results will bear healthy news and I will live out these truths.

I am prepped and being wheeled off to the surgical suite. The meds start to relax me and I drift off into thought.

Everything has to come back clean. I have so much life yet to live, so much to experience and to give.

I lie on the surgical table and tell the nurse how nervous I am about the pain and recovery. She reaches down to rub my arm and assures me it should be an easier recovery than the bilateral mastectomy. I hold on to that hope as I count backward from ten and fall asleep.

I wake up in recovery groggy with my stomach swirling. I have immediate flashbacks to my last surgery.

I don't want to throw up. I don't want to be in excruciating pain. I don't want to deal with the drains. I am afraid to look at my body in a mirror. This new body. These implants.

Due to my difficult recovery with the bilateral mastectomy, my doctors have me staying at the hospital overnight.

I lie in bed in my hospital room, sporting a pink surgical bra with a Velcro front closure, and an IV line coming out of my arm. I hold a vomit bag close to my face and a bottle of peppermint essential oil close to my nose. I do everything I can to settle my stomach and not throw up. I succeed, and I give a little smile to my nurses as my nausea fades.

The nurses and I settle into the all too familiar pattern of checking vitals, emptying and measuring my drains, and administering meds for both pain and nausea.

Thankfully the evening is uneventful, and I feel better than I'd anticipated when I wake up. I delight in the small joy of a cup of bad hospital coffee. I proudly take a selfie and post it to social media to share with my supportive community that I am well and ready to go home.

CLEAN (9/21/21)

It's been one week since surgery. I rapidly refresh my email again. I see a notification that my pathology results are available on the online portal. I want to open the message and I am also scared out of my fucking mind. I sit for a few minutes, and my leg shakes up and down as I debate whether to open it alone or with someone.

What if the cancer is still there? What if it has spread more? Should I wait to hear from the doctor or should I just open it now?

Throughout the past week, I have covered my fear with confidence. Confidence that all will be fine. It wasn't completely a false confidence. I do truly believe the results will be clean. But the reality remains, cancer has fucked with me before and I have to be prepared it may happen again.

I stare at the login screen of the online portal app. I need to know these results. I close my eyes, take a deep breath, say a little prayer, and open the message.

THIRTEEN LYMPH NODES REMOVED AND NO EVIDENCE OF METASTATIC CARCINOMA!

I read it again before I read the detailed report.

THIRTEEN LYMPH NODES REMOVED AND NO EVIDENCE OF METASTATIC CARCINOMA!

These are the best words I've received from a doctor in nearly nine months!

So why do the words fall so flat? Why am I not jumping for joy? Why am I not crying tears of happiness?

I walk upstairs to where Derek is working and show him the message on my phone screen.

Maybe his excitement will make me feel better?

The corners of his mouth turn up and he leaps out of this chair to hug me.

It doesn't change how I feel. Nothing changes within me.

I call my parents and sister with the results.

"Pathology came back with all thirteen lymph nodes clean," I relay.

"Oh, Amy! This is such wonderful news. The best news I've heard this year!" my dad says, filled with enthusiasm.

"Oh thank G-d, Amy. Thank G-d!" my mom adds with relief in her voice.

They are over the moon. I remain unemotional.

The call with my sister is much of the same.

Maybe when I speak to the doctor and hear her say the words, rather than me reading them, something will shift in me.

Nope. I hear the words repeated by both my breast surgeon and my oncologist and I still feel nothing.

Am I crazy? What the hell is going on here? Why aren't I more excited? Why do I still feel this tight pit in my stomach?

Over the next several days, I meditate and ask for guidance. In the stillness and quiet, I hear within me,

Yes, this is the best news…and…I still am not ready to celebrate.

What a fucking revelation! I can feel happy and scared at the same time!

I realize I am not ready to celebrate because:

- I still have a ways to go until I'll technically be finished with treatment and declared NED (No Evidence of Disease). This process consists of ten more infusion treatments over thirty weeks and twenty-five rounds of radiation over five weeks.

- Breast cancer has changed me. I wonder how long it will be until I'll be comfortable with my new body and whether I'll always see cancer when I take my bra off. I wonder whether I'll feel the same fear six months, and six years, from now.
- I never thought about a cancer diagnosis before December 2020. Now I do, and I remain worried about the future. If cancer returns or metastasizes, will I have to do all this shit all over again? The chemo, the treatments, and the emotions? Will I die? Will it kill me then?
- Cancer will forever be present in my life—the scars, the foobs (that's fake boobs for those who didn't know), the checkups, the mental and emotional wounds, and the fear of recurrence and possible additional surgeries.
- Too many women haven't heard, or won't get to hear, the good news I just received. A lot of guilt, sadness, and anger comes along with this fact.

So, am I happy with the pathology results? You better believe it.

And, I am still sad, scared, feeling guilty, and oh so fucking mad at cancer.

RADIATION: THE TECHNICAL SHIT

Today, Derek and I will meet with my radiation oncologist, Dr. Conner. When we arrive, we are taken to an exam room by Julie, who introduces herself as Dr. Conner's nurse.

"How are you doing today, Amy?" she asks as Derek and I take our seats.

"Mmmm. I'm okay," I reply. I'm too tired to be honest with her and tell her how I'm really feeling.

She takes my vitals and, at this point, I can pretty much recite the intake questions I know she will ask. We run through those, once again confirming my diagnosis, treatment so far, current meds and allergies, along with surgeries I've had to treat the cancer.

"Dr. Conner will be in shortly to see you. Go ahead and take off everything from the waist up and put on this gown please, so he can do a physical exam and check your skin," she says after wrapping up her portion of the appointment.

Another day, another doctor, and another gown.

I change and then Derek and I each look at our phones, a way to distract ourselves as we wait.

Dr. Conner comes in, pumps some sanitizer on his hands, rubs them together, and reintroduces himself with a warm smile. He hesitantly puts out his hand, takes it back, and puts out his fist instead, to give me a fist pump. Something one might typically consider odd for a doctor, but it has become a norm in these times of COVID so as not to shake hands.

"It's good to see you both again. It's been a while since we first met and a lot has happened since then. We have quite a bit to discuss today, but before we get started with any of that, how are you doing?"

The fatherly way in which he speaks makes me open up.

"Actually, I'm having a really hard time right now. There have been so many unexpected changes and I'm exhausted. I'm also still in a lot of discomfort from my exchange surgery and I have a lot of questions about this next step. Overall, I'm not doing so great, if I'm being completely honest."

One of hardest things about this fuckery is I barely have time to recover and process one trauma before I have to move on to the next.

He hands me a tissue, leans forward in his chair, which faces me, and says, "I can understand all of that, Amy. You have been through a lot and your body has been through a lot. As you know, when I initially met with Dr. Ramirez and Dr. Bender to review your case, we were unsure whether you'd need radiation. We discussed it a lot and we do believe it is the best plan. Remember though, all this is up to you. You call the shots here. How about we talk a bit about radiation and then see how you feel? Does that sound good?"

Wow! I feel like an actual human being here, not just "the next patient in room two."

I nod and look over at Derek as to question whether that sounds good to him too. In moments like this I wonder how he feels about all that has happened to his wife. He nods and Dr. Conner begins to talk about radiation and my specific treatment plan.

I take notes in my little green notebook.

He discusses the difference between photon (traditionally used) and proton (newer technology) therapy and shares that this facility is one of only a few to offer proton therapy. I listen intently as he reviews the pros and cons of each therapy. In the end, they are both safe and effective options.

He sighs and continues, "Typically, it is much more difficult, close to impossible, to get insurance companies to approve proton therapy. It is new and the equipment is still a lot more expensive so the insurance companies don't want to pay for that when they could pay less for a similar therapy, photon therapy. If you want to try for proton therapy, you have a unique opportunity."

He is making all this information very digestible, and my ears perk up even more when he mentions a unique opportunity.

"We are currently conducting a study to research the side effects and overall quality of life of people who receive breast cancer radiation. If you choose to participate in the study, you will be randomly chosen to receive either photon or proton therapy. The study will follow you for ten years and measure your quality of life throughout that time."

He continues to explain more about the study. While the choice is 100 percent up to me, unless I choose to put my name in the hat for the study, it is unlikely insurance will cover proton therapy. Dr. Conner will still try, of course, but it's very unlikely. I ask a few questions, such as how often I'll answer questionnaires and whether there is any penalty to drop out of the study at any point.

I am satisfied with his answers and really don't see any reason not to do the study. I think it will give me a sense of being a part of something bigger and a way to help others, so I am an easy yes.

"Okay great. The research team will contact you and soon after you are entered into the study, we will find out which therapy you will receive. For photon therapy, because the radiation will be to your left chest wall, we need a way to protect the radiation from reaching your heart. A technique called deep inspiration breath hold [DIBH] will be used for this. DIBH is not necessary for proton therapy as the beams stop before they reach any critical organs, such as the heart."

Deep inspiration breath hold is a radiation therapy technique where patients take a deep breath during treatment, and hold this breath while the radiation is delivered. By taking a deep breath in, your lungs fill with air and your heart will move away from your chest. DIBH can be useful in situations where radiation therapy is necessary in the chest region, and it is desired to avoid radiation dose to the heart (The Peter MacCallum Cancer Centre 2022).

He inches forward a bit in his seat and continues, "We need to do what's called mapping before you start radiation. Your radiation will be targeted to the left breast and chest wall, which extends from the collarbone to below the breast, as well as your underarm area. Before you leave today, Julie will schedule that appointment for you."

Protect from reaching my heart? I hadn't even thought about this.

Dr. Conner must sense my fear, as he pipes up and adds, "If you receive photon therapy, a monitor will be placed near your face that will light up green when your breath hold is in the right range. This is all based on the mapping we're going to do prior to treatment. If for any reason you let your breath go, the radiation will stop."

I release a nervous smile, nod, and continue to take notes.

Dr. Conner stops to confirm that I don't have any questions. I shake my head and tell him I'm good, and he then moves on to discuss some of the typical side effects of radiation therapy, which are skin irritation, skin burning, skin peeling, and fatigue.

Great, more fatigue. Just when I thought things were going to get better after chemo.

He checks my implants and the skin of my chest wall as a baseline. I'm happy to hear him say I'm healing well and my skin looks great post-surgery.

Radiation therapy will be every Monday to Friday for five weeks, for a total of twenty-five sessions. Once a week, I will see either Dr. Conner or the nurse practitioner for a skin check and overall check-in.

We have been here for over an hour and the exhaustion shows on my body and face, which Dr. Conner recognizes and honors.

"We've discussed a lot today. As long as you don't have any other questions, I'll step out so you can get dressed. Julie will come back in a few minutes to schedule your mapping appointment and then you can get going."

I look to Derek and back to Dr. Conner. "I think we're good for today. You good, Derek?" He confirms and, with a smile, Dr. Conner pumps hand sanitizer in his palm and leaves the exam room.

Julie returns a few minutes later, and we schedule my mapping appointment and head out. I release a deep sigh as we walk to the car. This is all just too much. Yet, I must forge ahead. For me, for my kids, and for the tremendous amount of life I know I have left to live.

The next few days are focused on rest and slow walks as I continue to heal from my exchange surgery. I relish in the fact that I can take longer walks and spend more time with my kids without as much fatigue. I also know the fatigue may return with radiation. I remind myself nothing is permanent—not the fatigue nor the cancer.

While Derek has attended many appointments with me, I figure the mapping will be easy so I go by myself. I drive with the music loud and try to focus on anything other than cancer. I'm greeted in the lobby by a young man, who introduces himself as John, who will be helping with the mapping today. As expected, I'm directed to a changing room, where I take off everything from the waist up and don a green gown.

We then move to a room with what looks like it could be a radiation machine. John explains it is similar but does not emit any radiation. This machine is used only for the purpose of mapping out the radiation area.

"How is your range of motion since your surgery?" he asks while getting me situated on the table.

"It's okay, but still not great. I've been going to physical therapy and stretching at home too."

"Do you think you can keep your arms held overhead for an hour without moving?" he asks with hesitation in his voice.

"An hour? Nobody told me this would take that long. I don't know if I'll be able to do that. I still have a lot of pain in that position."

Just then, Dr. Conner walks in and our conversation stops.

"How are you doing today, Amy?" he asks in his upbeat voice.

"Doing okay. A little nervous as John just told me about holding my arms up for an hour. I don't know if I can do that," I reply with tears in my eyes.

"Let's see. Go ahead and place your arms overhead for me."

I do, and I can tell by the look he exchanges with John that it's not good.

"You really need to be able to stretch a bit higher. I want you to continue with physical therapy and come back in a week. You should be good to go then. I won't be here, but my colleague Dr. Kim will be. We all work together and she will take good care of you. I promise."

The tears leave my eyes, run down my cheeks, and reach my face mask. I am afraid this will put my treatment outside of the optimal time frame. Dr. Conner assures me we will still be on track.

I leave very upset, not just at the situation but also at myself. If only I had worked harder at PT or done more exercises at home, maybe I wouldn't be in this position. It is another bump in this road that I never wanted to be on in the first place. I know it isn't that big of a deal, but right now my emotions are hot and heavy. I don't know how much more I can take.

Over the next week, I work hard on my range of motion with extra stretches in addition to my scheduled physical therapy. I want to be 100 percent ready when I return.

I nervously drive back to the main cancer center where the radiation office is. I pull into the dark parking garage and breathe deeply to calm myself.

John greets me in the lobby once again and walks me back to the mapping room. It is déjà vu of last week. Once I'm on the table, he begins marking Xs on various parts of my chest wall.

Just then, a woman walks in.

"Hi, Amy. I'm Dr. Kim. As Dr. Conner told you, I'll be doing your mapping today. I know you had some range of motion issues last week. Let's see how you're doing today."

I inhale deeply, close my eyes, and raise my arms above my head as I exhale.

Please say I'm all good. Please.

"This looks great, Amy! You've really made progress this week. You are in a great spot to move ahead today," she says with a smile that expands behind her mask.

I breathe a sigh of relief.

She reviews what the appointment entails. She will be using CT scanning to precisely locate the treatment fields and create a "map," which will be used to design the treatment to fit my specific case. She also reminds me about the deep inspiration breath hold, and then asks if I have any questions.

"Nope. Let's do this. I'm ready."

She goes into a small room and a nurse comes in to double-check John's work. The nurse explains that she will be marking these areas with minute tattoos, which Dr. Conner had told me about.

These will be my first ever tattoos. Yes, they're real tattoos. I look and they are so incredibly small I can't even see them. The tattoos will serve as permanent markers for treatment that won't wash away when I shower. I could have opted for nonpermanent markings and had them done more often throughout radiation. The other cool thing they do during this visit is make an "immobilization form," or body mold, of my upper body. This will be used during radiation to ensure I am lying in the exact same position every time. It is all very precise, as it should be. Scans, molds, and tattoos, oh my!

With my arms raised in position, I lie on the table and wait. I soon hear Dr. Kim's voice over the speaker, and she instructs me when to breathe, when to hold, and when to release.

I am still quite sore in the underarm scar area, where the breast surgeon performed the axillary lymph node dissection only weeks earlier. I know I want to get this done, though. I need to get this done.

After about an hour, Dr. Kim comes back in.

"You did great Amy. We got everything we need for this step. Go ahead and bring your arms down."

"Oh, thank goodness!" I sigh as I slowly move my arms down. They have become a bit numb over the past hour from the lack of movement.

I change back into my clothes and leave the dressing room.

Before leaving the office, the nurse gives me my radiation schedule. I will begin on Wednesday, November 3, 2021, or so I think.

RADIATION: THE EMOTIONAL BURNS (11/3/21–12/14/21)

It's day one and I am a nervous wreck. I've had so much anxiety leading up to this first treatment. I'll be receiving the photon therapy, and as much as Dr. Conner has prepared me, it's another thing I have never done so I still don't fully know what to expect. Thankfully, Derek is with me to keep me calm and offer support and love.

I check in and find a seat in the waiting room. My nerves shake and my heart beats fast. A woman dressed in scrubs comes out to the waiting room and calls me back.

"Hi Amy. I'm Alison. I'm one of the three radiation technicians who will be part of your team," she says with a smile.

I walk by her side, down a hallway, which seems to stretch on forever. My nerves build with every step. These white walls are ever expansive with beautiful artwork throughout. I wonder if they put this seemingly bright and cheery art here to help take our minds off what is happening behind the doors of these rooms. I am reminded of my thoughts surrounding the room I was taken to when Dr. Dallas told me I'd need the biopsies. It seems like forever ago.

We pass several people along the way, and we exchange smiles, in solidarity of one another. I wonder what type of cancer they have and how many radiation treatments, if any, they have already been through. I wonder if they had to endure chemo, like me. I am still pretty bald, so my chemo and cancer remain very visible.

Alison pushes open a door, which leads us to a large dressing room.

"Every day when you get here, you'll come in and grab an upper body gown. You'll get changed and go to the next waiting room to be called back," she says as she pulls a gown out of the closet.

It looks like the crop top of hospital gowns, which causes me to chuckle, as it's quite fashionable.

"Today, you're not receiving treatment. Your actual treatment will begin tomorrow."

I raise my eyebrows and give her a questioning look.

"What? I'm not starting radiation today?" I say with a lot of confusion and frustration in my voice.

What is she talking about? Today was day one on the treatment calendar they gave me.

"No. Didn't they tell you today is a simulation? Now that your plan has been created, we need to make sure everything they've created in the system lines up with the imaging and markers. So it'll be the same process as radiation, you'll be on the table that you'll be on for treatment, you just won't be receiving the actual treatment today."

Is she telling me I just spent all this energy worrying, and today isn't even the actual first day? I can't believe I was not told this information! Seems like an important piece.

After a deep breath, I explain no one had informed me of this and I expected today to be day one of treatment. She apologizes more than once while slowly and hesitantly handing me the gown.

I am irritated as I take the gown and enter changing room number four. I wiggle myself out of my shirt and then my bra. Standing topless in this room, I see my chest reflected in the full-length mirror, and the reason why I am here hits me like a ton of bricks. Sadness and anger flood my body. I want to cry, but don't have the energy. I wasted it all on worrying.

I consider this yet another nod from the Universe reminding me that no matter how much I worry, I still cannot control the outcome of things in this life. I can hear this a million times and worry still has its way of seeping in through the cracks.

I slide my arms through the sleeves, take a deep breath, and with a pit in my belly, I walk the few steps from the dressing room to the next waiting room.

A few minutes later, Alison meets me there.

"You ready?" she asks, a little too cheerful for me right now.

I shrug my shoulders and reply, "Guess so. Let's do this."

We walk to a small room attached to the actual radiation room.

She explains that I will come to this same room each day. She then introduces me to two other techs and tells me the three of them will be my radiation team throughout my treatments. The thought of having a team brings me comfort, as I'll see the same people each day. And a team is made up of people who are cheering for you, which brings a smile to my face. This smaller room is somewhat like an office and appears very technical with a lot of computers and various screens. Right there, one of the screens displays my face and one of the images of my chest wall taken during mapping. It shows where the radiation is to be administered.

"Every day, when we get in this room, you'll tell us your full name, birthday, and the area we're radiating. Then we'll go into the radiation room," Alison explains. I stand there uncomfortably, in my leggings, Uggs, and medical crop top.

She leads me into the radiation room. A large exam table sits in the middle of the room, with the radiation machine attached to it. Several cameras and lights hang from the ceiling. She has me lie down on the table and take my gown off. She then covers my lower half with a warm blanket. I welcome the comfort, considering how cold it is in the room and on the table—a bit of a spa feeling in what is definitely not a spa treatment room.

Alison and Ron, one of the other techs on my team, work together to position me. It all must be exactly precise. I lie still while they tug different ways at the sheet beneath me. It is really quite uncomfortable. My body feels crooked at the hips. All this is being done while my arms are raised above my head, my hands in a prayer position, and my chin is tilted up and to the right.

Once I'm positioned correctly, Ron looks directly at me and says, "Amy, it is really important you lie completely still throughout the imaging process. Every time you move, we will likely have to start that image over, which means a longer process for you. We don't want you to stay in this position any longer than you have to."

They both leave the room and return to the first, smaller room where Kristy, the third tech on my team, is.

I hear Alison through a speaker, "Okay, Amy. You're great, just like that. We're going to get started, so be sure to lie completely still and listen for the cues to hold your breath."

My chest tightens and my heart pounds. I wonder how long this will take and whether I can actually do it.

The team is really great as they guide me over the microphone throughout the imaging.

Despite them assuring me all is going well, I can feel a panic attack coming on. It feels like I've been on this table for hours, and I don't like not knowing how much time has passed. It is all awful and scary: the intermittent flashing bulbs like a camera flash, the sounds I've never heard before, the beeping, being stuck in a very uncomfortable position knowing I can't move, seeing my reflection in the glass of the radiation machine, and wondering if I am holding my breath correctly.

I am in so much fucking pain. My upper arms tingle and have become numb due to being overhead for so long. It gets worse with every minute I'm on this table. I feel the worst pins and needles, plus the worst itching and burning feeling, and I can't move or do anything about it.

I want to squirm. I want to scream.

Ron comes in to change something with the machine and I start to cry. I just can't take this.

"I'm in so much pain. My arms really hurt, like nothing I've felt before. Can I put them down for just a minute while you're in here?"

"I know it's uncomfortable. Unfortunately, if you move, we'll have to start all over as it will change your positioning," he says in a warm and kind tone.

I definitely don't want to do that. I feel so trapped right now.

His head tilted to the side, raised eyebrows, and smile all convey he feels bad this is happening.

"I could try to scratch or rub your arm while you stay in position, if you think it might help."

I accept the offer and he helps as much as he can before returning to the other room so we can continue the simulation and finish this as quickly as possible.

"You're doing great. Just a little bit longer. I know it's hard," he says as he leaves the room.

Something about him walking back out of the room leaves me feeling so alone. I can see my chest in the glass of the radiation machine. I feel so exposed and vulnerable. Not in an "Oh shit, I'm naked in front of people" sort of way, but in a "Holy shit, this cancer is still real and I am going to have radiation, right here on this table" sort of way. I lie still. Tears run their course down my cheeks. I offer up a silent prayer and faithfully trust these invisible beams will kill any rogue cancer cells. Cancer is literally staring me down as I look at my breast in the reflection. My new breast and chest, all marked up. My new breast with no nipple, that is. I am once again reminded my body is forever changed. I sob while trying to remain still.

The more I cry, the more anxious I feel, and the more anxious I feel, the more I cry. I want this vicious cycle to stop. In the past, I've relied on visualization to help calm me, so I close my eyes and try to picture myself on a beach. As I think about the sand, my body itches even more. Ugh!

I mentally ground down through my feet and think about an episode of *Ted Lasso* where Ted is having a panic attack and Rebecca is telling him to "just breathe" (Lowney 2020, 26:50). So, in between the techs coaching me through DIBH, I practice slow breaths. I successfully calm myself and make it through.

Alison and Ron return to the room and both cheer, "You did it! Great job!"

They help me off the table. My arms are completely numb. Alison assures me it should get better now they are out of that position.

She walks me back to the dressing room. I return to dressing room number four, change back into my clothes, and head out to the main lobby where Derek has been waiting.

"Well, it wasn't even the first one," I say with a smirk and explain it all to him.

He hugs me tightly.

We return for the actual day one and continue from there, day by day, Monday to Friday for five weeks, for a total of twenty-five treatments. Unfortunately, the anxiety, pain, and loneliness I felt during the simulation accompanies me to most of these appointments.

I'm reminded of other times throughout this cancer fuckery. No matter how much incredible support I receive and no matter the number of people by my side, physically and literally, I can still feel so alone. The fact remains I am the only one actually in the weeds of it all. People can say all the things to make me feel like they are in it with me, but they aren't, and that feels very isolating at times.

Some days I lie on the radiation table and everything is just procedural to me. Other days it is more emotional, and these are the harder days. At times, it feels I could be at one of many doctor appointments for anything. Gastro, gyno, general doctor—any of them. Another day, another appointment. It has become what I do, like eating, sleeping, or brushing my teeth. I'm aware some of this is a survival mechanism.

And then I snap back to reality. The big "c" word returns to the forefront of my mind. I am not just standing in any dressing room, putting on any medical gown, as I've done countless times in my lifetime. I am in the radiation wing of the cancer center, putting on a gown that, for fuck's sake, is pink. Really, people? Enough with the pink! It all floods back. I have breast cancer and I am here in an attempt to kill any remaining cancer cells that may have decided they want to hang out in my body a little longer for some reason.

On day ten of twenty-five, I am overwhelmed with sadness and anger toward cancer. It has been a crazy eleven months and some days it just becomes too much. As I drive to radiation, I allow these emotions to flow out of me. I scream at the top of my lungs to let them out. When I get to radiation, I am quieter than usual. I just want today's treatment to be over with so I can go home and crawl back into bed.

When I finish treatment, I walk back out to the main lobby, just as I have the past ten times. As I get closer to the exit, I do a double take. My beautiful sister Leigh is sitting in the lobby! She comes up and gives me the biggest hug and I just sob in her arms, right there in the lobby. I am a blubbering mess, audibly crying, I can't catch my breath, my nose is likely running, and I don't even care there are people all around us to witness this. It is a true moment of vulnerability for me. I allow myself to feel and show what cancer is truly about.

"What are you doing here?" I deeply inhale and ask her.

"I just knew. I woke up this morning and knew we both needed each other," she says as she squeezes me tightly.

She is 100 percent right. It is exactly what I need. My sister. Hugs. Love. I am so grateful she lives less than an hour away and can show up for me like this. We go out for coffee and breakfast, and the time together is like gold.

I continue through the treatments and am surprised by the overall mental exhaustion. Going to radiation Monday to Friday, having cancer slapped in my face constantly, takes its toll on me. To help with this, I listen to uplifting music or a podcast on the drive to and from treatments. Many days I treat myself to a latte and a delicious treat from my favorite gluten-free bakery. I remember I am going through a lot and deserve treats and moments to find joy in the little things! And yes, I understand about sugar and cancer. I also believe everything in moderation, and if a latte and scone are what it takes, I say do it!

I am more than halfway through my twenty-five radiation treatments and my parents are in town for Thanksgiving. We meet for breakfast one morning after my radiation treatment and, as we sit waiting for our food, they ask me how I am doing.

Sitting in that booth, with strangers at tables on both sides of me, I really do not want to be hysterical, but I just can't stop the tears from coming.

"I feel so broken! I hate going to radiation every damn day. And, as if that's not bad enough, all of a sudden I can't stop thinking about all that has happened this past year. I don't know what to do. I feel so lost. I don't even recognize myself. This isn't me. I've never been the person who thinks negatively, but I can't help it. I'll be driving down the road and the thought will pop in my head, 'What if I had died? My kids may not have had a mom.' I think about how the cancer could come back and what I would do then. How I couldn't take it all again. I don't want to be this person. I want to go back to being me. Regular, positive me, who is excited to be alive. I've called a therapist, but other than that, I just don't know what else to do. I'm so sorry to lay this all on you here, but I just need to get it out."

"You may never be the same person, Amy. This experience has been such a big part of your life. I'm glad you told us and that you've reached out to a therapist. Hopefully they can share some ideas with you, to help you as you move forward," my mom says.

My dad then adds, "It's more than okay that you feel this way. While I haven't been through what you have, this all seems normal, especially now chemo is over and you have more time and space to think about these things."

As we sit and talk, it becomes apparent to me I will likely never be the same person. This line in the sand has come to define pre-cancer and post-cancer Amy. Perhaps I do not need to go back to that former version of myself. Like the butterfly, I needed this cocoon—although it is a shitty one!—to transform into a more beautiful soul.

December rolls in with a beautiful sunny day, albeit a cold one. I bundle up in my many layers, a hat, and gloves. After walking for about fifteen minutes, I feel a layer of sweat inside my gloves. I take them off and quickly wish I hadn't. It is bitterly cold. I almost put the gloves back on but decide not to. I want to feel the cold on my body. After having been through such hardship, I am indeed alive. I can feel cold air.

Physically, radiation hasn't been too bad for me, until now, as I enter my final week. My underarm area has become red and itchy. I feel really lucky to have had this experience, as I know it could have been much worse.

Leading up to radiation, I wish I'd heard less of "The hard part is over" and "Radiation is so much easier than chemo." Statements like these had me walking into this step of treatment expecting it to be easy breezy. I'm pretty sure someone even referred to it as such in conversation.

Radiation was not easier than chemo. It was not a breeze. It was a different kind of hard.

With chemo, I had time in between treatments. With radiation, it was every damn day. Side effects from radiation were much easier than chemo. Both are a different kind of hard: physically, emotionally, and mentally.

I decide to ring the bell after my last radiation. It feels different completing radiation, as it truly is the end of this step.

I am officially done with radiation and the bell is a way to mark that. I grab the rope and give it a good tug. The ringing is super loud, which takes me by surprise and makes me chuckle a bit. It feels good to smile, laugh, and *be done*!

Derek and I share lots of hugs and celebrate with a delicious breakfast. I've learned it is so important to celebrate every win along this path. While the physical side effects of radiation itself weren't anything like chemo, it has been hard as fuck emotionally. Even though these scars are not visible on my body, I am certain they will never leave me.

FORGED BY FIRE (12/12/21)

Meals have been ordered and mimosas delivered to the table. It's been a couple of weeks since I've seen Layton and we have a lot to catch up on, as we typically don't go this long without seeing each other. My emotions have been on fire and I need the support of my bestie. I am so grateful to have this time with her.

"How are you?" asks Layton.

Some people just want to hear "I'm fine" when they ask this question, but I know she wants the real answer, and I know I want and need to give it to her.

"I'm a mess."

As she always does, she invites me to say more. It's one of the ways I know she's my best friend because she truly wants to know what has me feeling this way.

I share how it seems like I'm experiencing this crazy wave of emotions now that chemo and radiation are over. I finally have a chance to come up for air, a moment to breathe, and am now facing the trauma my body and mind have endured over the past eleven months. Both my oncologist and therapist had told me PTSD in breast cancer patients has been proven in studies, so I haven't been completely surprised by these feelings of anxiety and depression.

With tears welling up, I lean in and tell her, "I feel totally broken. I don't know if I'll ever be the same optimistic person I've always been and that makes me really sad. This entire experience has rocked me."

I am reminded of a gift my sister gave me shortly after I was diagnosed, a beautiful pewter heart charm with a crack in it that has been sealed by embossment. The charm is called "Perfectly Imperfect" and the accompanying card shares about the Japanese art form Kintsugi. Kintsugi is the art of treating breakage and repair as part of the history of an object, rather than something to disguise, by mending the broken areas of pottery and ceramics. In this philosophy, the Japanese are able to find beauty and value in the brokenness (Kelly Richman-Abdou 2022).

I have dealt with anxiety and depression since I was a teenager, so I have certainly felt broken before. This time feels different. In past instances, I had some control over what was causing the feelings. With cancer, I haven't had that control. I see my scars in the mirror and feel ugly and tarnished. I've lost my sense of self and my way in the world, causing deep shame. I question who I am, what I am worth, and how this cancer fuckery will impact the rest of my life. None of this has been up to me and I am furious.

Layton knows all this and she isn't here to fix the situation at hand. She is here to bear witness to my pain. To sit in it with me and be a mirror for me.

With a smile, she boldly says, "You're not going to be the same person, Amy. This is going to change you forever. But I believe it's made you into an even better version of yourself. Anyone can say they are a glass half full person and then lose that view through a traumatic event. You didn't lose it. You moved through this with strength and grace, showing people that all this can't stop you."

"So I didn't lose my spark?" I ask, and then share the earlier conversation I'd had with Jen about how her biggest fear was I'd lose my spark.

I have been thinking so much about this and really feeling ashamed. Have I lost my spirit? Have I lost what people love about me? What I love about myself? What makes me me?

"No, you didn't lose it! You basically threw gasoline all over that shit. You are more on fire now than ever before. You were always going to make an impact and talk to people about the power of optimism. Now you have this story to make it all even more impactful. You've been forged by fire, Amy."

Seeing myself through her lens, I realize my brokenness doesn't have to tarnish me. It can make me shine brighter. I once saw Gabby Bernstein quote in an Instagram post, "A disco ball is hundreds of pieces of broken glass put together to make a magical ball of light. You're not broken. You're a disco ball," (Gabrielle Bernstein, 2021).

I will try to embrace my broken pieces.

I get home from brunch and grab my journal and my favorite purple felt-tip pen.

* * *

Journal Entry 12/12/21

I used to think that if I felt the sadness or the anger, I wasn't being the positive, optimistic person everyone knew me to be. Through this cancer journey, I've learned that not only is it okay to feel these emotions but it is also necessary! And on top of that, doing so doesn't make me any less of a positive person.

We are human. Humans have emotions. We must honor them.

Without the darkness, we cannot see and appreciate the light.

Without the bad, we cannot see and appreciate the good.

Without the negative, we cannot see and appreciate the positive.

Allow yourself to feel all *the feelings. Sit with them. Process them. Don't fight them. Be at peace with them.*

THE WONDERING AND TURNING WITHIN (2/10/22)

Rib pain.

Sternum pain.

Headaches.

I call the oncologist and she orders a bone scan and brain MRI.

And yesterday I noticed heavy bruising on my leg. I don't remember bumping it on anything. In the past, I would've thought Derek kicked me during the night in his sleep, but now I wonder.

And today, I'm pretty sure I got my period. I haven't had my period since starting chemo eleven months ago. The meds had stopped my period. Dr. Ramirez had told me that based on my age there was a fifty-fifty chance it would return. After already enduring perimenopausal shit, I really was hopeful this bleeding was that. If it's my period, I'll have to go through natural menopause and do all that shit again. Oh, the hot flashes! I let out a muttered scream. It's muttered because I'm not alone in the house and don't want to scare anyone.

Before cancer, all these things would have been exactly what they are. Pains, aches, marks, and blood.

Now, I worry.

Is cancer in my bones?
My lungs?
My brain?
My blood?
Is it my period or is this something else? Something more serious? Is this a sign of ovarian cancer or uterine cancer?

On their own each of these could be nothing, but combined? Fuck, is it back?

Could it be the implants?
Do I have breast implant illness?
Are the fucking implants making my autoimmune issues worsen?

I am spiraling. I can barely function.

I've been having trouble staying on task or getting motivated to write for some time now. Today, I have been so damn tired. I take a short walk, hopeful the fresh air will help. I look around and notice how beautiful the sky is. I touch a tree to connect with nature. It is a good reminder that we are all interconnected and life is cyclical. It feels good to be outside and clear my head of all the craziness. But I return home exhausted. My body aches. My eyes hurt.

How can I be so damn tired when I slept over eight hours last night?

I am completely drained. My body and my mind are bombed. This is a realization I've had to come to in the past, yet somehow I still forget.

I forget how much my body, my mind, my emotions, and my insides all work overtime. They have been for quite some time now. Not only this year of cancer fuckery but also the two plus years of having COVID in our world, of having our entire family home for so long while the world shut down for the pandemic on top of years of dealing with chronic pain and fatigue.

I take time to remember all this. I sit with it. I breathe. I forgive myself for all the "shoulds" I put on myself lately. *"I should be getting work done. I should take a walk today. I should write."*

I listen to my body. I lie still, close my eyes, place one hand on my heart and one on my belly, and I turn inward.

I breathe deeply.

I listen to the voice, the knowing within.

I hear:

"Yes, you are on a deadline, Amy. You need to write, but forcing it isn't the way to do that. If you don't make the deadline, *there will still be another opportunity. It is okay. You are tired. You need rest."*

And then:

"Write about exactly this experience. People need this. They need to hear this. Capture it now and then rest, sweet one."

LAST HP TREATMENT (3/30/22)

Today is my final treatment of Herceptin and Perjeta. It is hopefully the last time I will receive any medications for breast cancer. Hopefully the last time my port will be accessed and I will be able to have it removed soon.

I have been on autopilot for so long and can't help but wonder, "Now what?" Every end means a new beginning. What will this new beginning look like for me?

For today, I will focus on celebrating the end of this part of the process. It has been a very long road and I'm glad today is here.

I joked with Leigh that maybe I would wear a tiara. Last week I received a surprise package from her in the mail. It was a beautiful silver tiara with purple gemstones—my favorite color. I have never in my life worn a tiara, that I can recall, but I will wear it today.

I saw a shirt last week that said "It's All about the Journey" and I knew it would be perfect to wear today. With my special shirt on and my tiara in hand, I know I want to bring some other things with me today. Throughout the cancer fuckery, I have received many bracelets and necklaces with encouraging words on them. While I can't possibly wear all of them today, I've decided to put them all in a jewelry bag and bring them with me. This will be my special way of having with me each of the people who gifted the bracelets to me. I also grab a few of my favorite crystals, and then Derek and I hit the road for Dr. Ramirez's office.

When I'm called back to the infusion suite, the nurse leads me to the first bay. It is decorated with banners and weighted silver confetti centerpieces on each side table. I immediately feel special. Each nurse comes by to congratulate me.

Derek takes a few pictures of me, as I proudly sport my tiara and hold the confetti displays with a huge grin on my face. I am glad I don't have to wear a mask in the bay so my smile can be captured on camera.

We have a slight scare when my lead nurse Maria says, "I see you had COVID recently. Have you had a negative test since then?"

"Um, no. I had it almost two weeks ago. I didn't even think to take another test before coming today," I reply with my eyebrows raised.

She will need to check what the current protocol is.

Maria leaves the bay and I turn to Derek, half laughing, half worried. "Oh my g-d. What if I can't get my final treatment today. That would totally suck!"

She quickly returns and tells us we are good to go since it has been more than ten days. We all breathe a sigh of relief.

And with that, my final treatment begins.

Port accessed.

Saline flush.

Name and birthday recited.

Herceptin numbers called out by Maria and confirmed by Linda.

Herceptin hung on IV pole and drip started.

This is it. My last Herceptin.

About thirty minutes later, we hear the beep sounding the end of Herceptin.

Saline flush.

I'm ready for Perjeta when Maria tells me I have a special visitor.

I think it's either Layton, my parents, or my sister.

The door opens and I see my beautiful sister. She is carrying a gorgeous bouquet of flowers, two smiley face balloons and a gigantic dragonfly balloon. The dragonfly is my spirit animal. We both cry and she wants to get a couple of pictures of us with the balloons and flowers. She only stays with us for a few minutes and then heads back to the lobby to wait for me to finish.

With the balloons and flowers placed on a nearby chair, it's time to start Perjeta. Maria and a couple of other nurses ask me if I'm going to ring the bell when I finish today. I still don't know. I will have to see how I feel in the moment.

Perjeta runs for about thirty minutes.

Beep.

Saline flush.

And then I hear it. The last beep I will hear from this fucking IV machine.

I feel so victorious. Suddenly, I know I will ring that damn bell.

I did it. Take that, cancer. Take that!

Maria deaccesses my port and places a Band-Aid on it.

"That's it, Amy! You are finished! Do you want to ring the bell?" she says with excitement.

"Yes! Can my sister come back for that?"

I am glad to hear her say yes. It only seems right Leigh be here for this moment.

I walk to the bell. The entire office staff surrounds me. I'm not sure I like all the attention on me.

Amy, this moment is for you. Focus on you.

I grab hold of the bell and ring the shit out of it. My other arm lifts to the sky in triumph. Tears begin to fall, as I shout, "I did it! I did it!"

Everyone congratulates me and both Derek and Leigh give me hugs. Tears flow all around. I hope my hugs speak the words I can't, to thank them for how they have shown up for me over these past fifteen months.

The three of us meet Layton for lunch at one of my favorite restaurants to celebrate. Our time together is full of joy, laughter, and a lot of love.

It doesn't take long before the emotions settle in. My stomach rumbles. My palms are clammy. My head is swimming.

Every end means a new beginning.
What does this new beginning mean and look like for me?
Now is the beginning of healing—not the end of cancer at all.
It is time to accept all that's happened.
I've been on autopilot for so long.
Now what?
I want to feel happy today that this part is over.
Why can't I just feel happy?
It doesn't seem fair.
I don't even know why I'm crying.
Maybe they're happy tears.
Maybe the rumbling in my tummy is excitement rather than anxiety, but it doesn't feel that way.

AFTERSHOCK (12/28/21)

It's Tuesday night. The kids are at their various sports practices, and I am at home cooking dinner. I stare blankly at the vegetables sautéing in the pan. I am stuck in a loop of thoughts about all I have been through, all cancer has taken from me, and all cancer has mysteriously gifted me.

Around the corner is 2022. What will it bring? Will this time of year, the anniversary of my mammograms, biopsies, and diagnosis, always be tough for me?

My eyes begin to burn and then water, and not from the onions.

I fall to the floor and curl up in a ball. My body shakes like an earthquake. My tears are a rainstorm.

I am hysterical. Uncontrollable crying. I let it all flow out.

The emotions can come out of nowhere lately. I'll feel fine one day, and the next I'm thinking about what happens if cancer is still in my body or if it returns.

I think about how I don't want to die.

This is not the first time these unwelcome thoughts have overwhelmed me and these feelings have taken over my body.

I am learning the heavy weight of trauma. The uncertainty it carries.

Every ache. Every pain. Every scan. Every checkup.

I will never know why cancer chose me. And, as much as I want to, I know I do not need to understand it all.

This morning, I shared my feelings in RAW, my journaling community. I couldn't help but smile when these beautiful women held space for me to grieve and process. A genuine smile. A smile filled with love and joy.

I have so much to be grateful for. I am grateful for my health, for my family, for my support system, and for my fucking life!

I am not naive. I know this is not the end of cancer. Cancer will be part of my life forever. I hope that as the years go by, it becomes less raw and not a daily conscious thought.

No matter what the future brings, I know my smile no longer serves as armor. I no longer need to hide my feelings.

We all deserve to understand and feel a full, healthy range of emotions.

We deserve nourishing love and support.

We deserve safe, sacred spaces to be ourselves and bare it all.

PHOTOS FROM THE FUCKERY

Leigh and me at the beach before my bilateral mastectomy.

Chemo round one—sporting the gloves, frozen water bottles, and ice pack under my feet.

My dad cuts my hair.

A couple of the ponytails—thirteen inches were chopped off.

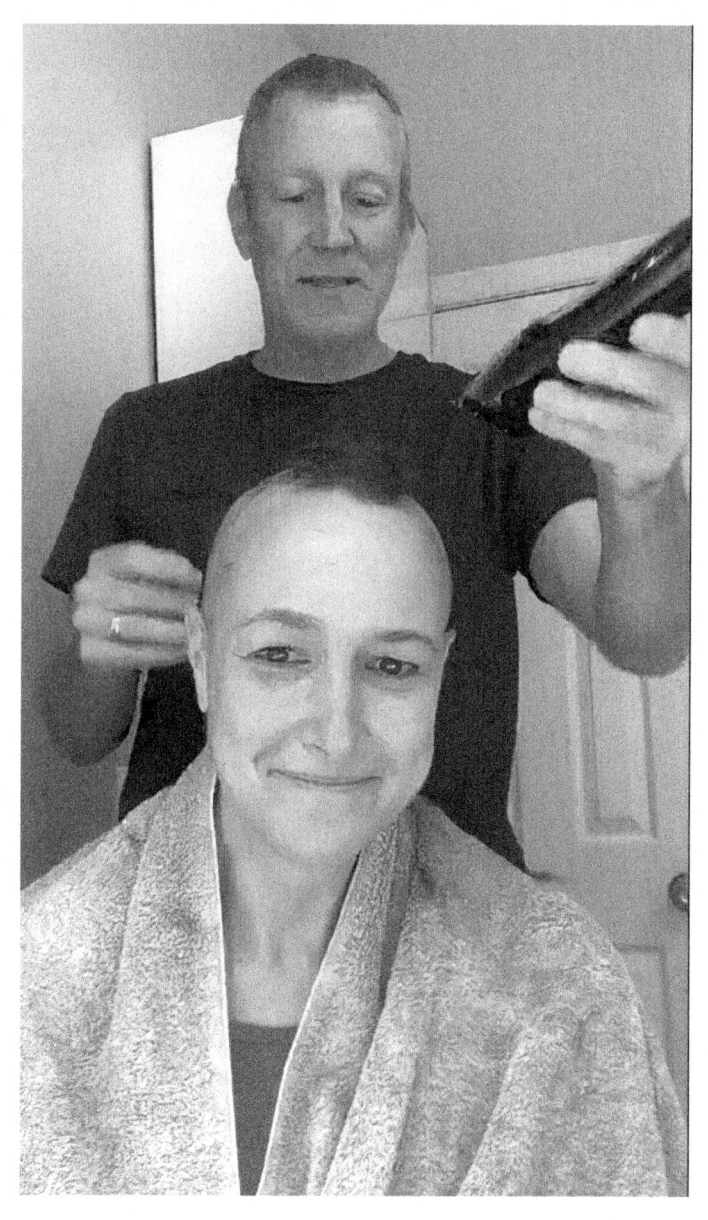

Derek shaving my head, live on Facebook.

The day we brought Tess home.

*Selfie in Corolla, North Carolina,
during our family beach vacation. I made it!*

PHOTOS FROM THE FUCKERY · **307**

Mom and me at chemo.

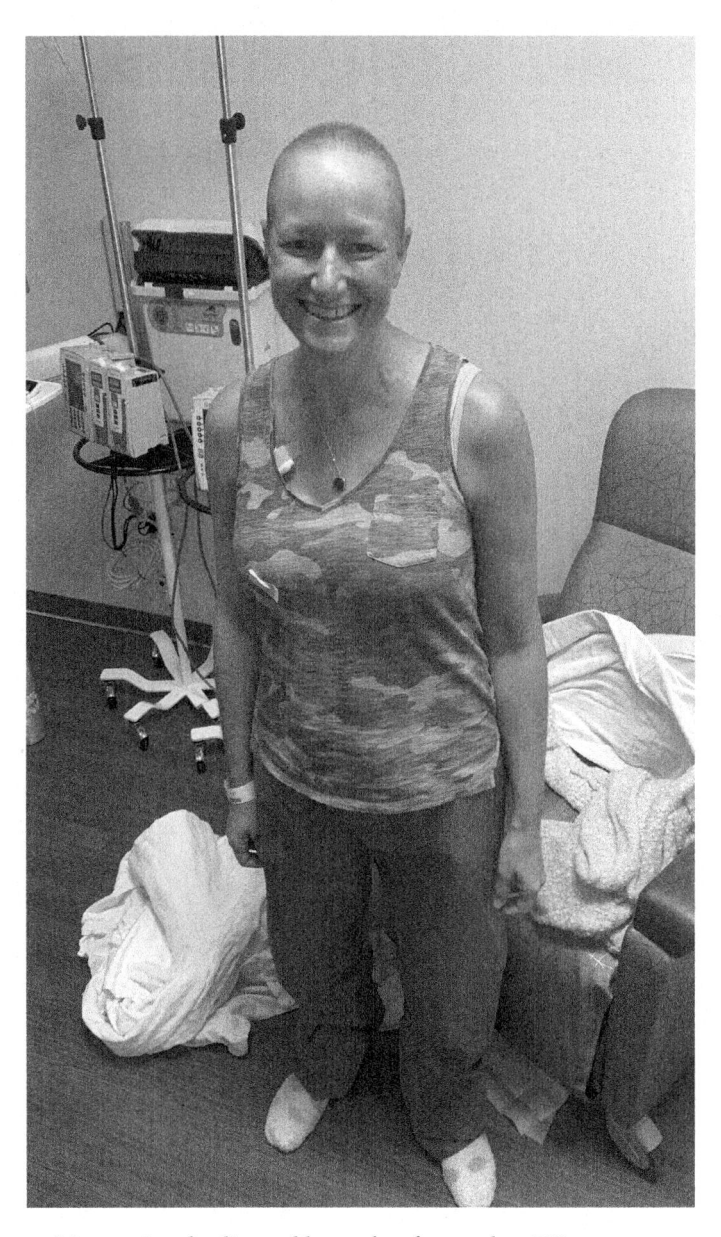

Me sporting the disposable scrubs after my last TC treatment and allergic reaction.

Me ringing the bell after completing twenty-five rounds of radiation.

Leigh and me with the balloons she brought when she surprised me during my last HP treatment.

PHOTOS FROM THE FUCKERY · 311

Me ringing the bell after completing my last HP treatment.

Layton and me at lunch after my last HP treatment.

A LOVE LETTER TO MY FAMILY

Dear Derek, Andrew, Jacob, Zachary, Dad, Mom, and Leigh,

Crisis can tear apart relationships or make them even stronger. Some moments throughout my cancer fuckery brought out the best and others the worst in all of us. Cancer affects not only the patients but also those who care so much about us.

Dad, at times I could look in your eyes and feel your sadness. Mom, I could hear the desperation in your voice as you wanted so badly to do anything you could to help your daughter. Derek, I felt the fear in your silence when we'd enter yet another doctor's office. Leigh, I could feel love, hope, and heartbreak as you watched and walked alongside your only sister and your best friend. We had moments of laughter, tears, rage, and gratitude. There were gifts received and lessons learned. In many ways, I believe cancer brought me closer to each of you, and for that I am forever grateful.

Derek, you have been a rock for our family and for me. We weren't in the greatest place when cancer invaded our life, and as promised, you stood by my side no matter what. The love, tenderness, patience, and support you provided are all reasons why I love you. You had to juggle so much during this and you did it without putting any of the burden on me. You helped me set healthy boundaries, some that should have been set years ago. I will never understand what any of this has been like for you and I pray I never have to. You are an incredible human being, Derek, and no matter what life brings us, I will always love you.

Andrew, Jacob, and Zachary, my sweet, beautiful boys. I need you to know that it breaks my heart you had to experience any of this. At the same time, I know deep inside, you've each learned important lessons that will come in handy at some time in your life. You may not see them now, but they are there. I'm sorry for all the times I couldn't do what you asked of me because I was too tired or felt too sick. I hate that I missed out on an entire year of your lives. I missed hockey, basketball, and baseball games, playing with you, doing homework with you, and simply being with you. You don't talk at all about your mom having breast cancer, how it impacted you, or what you felt. I hope someday you will open up and share more with me. I love you so deeply and I thank you for putting up with all the times I ask for another hug, kiss, or snuggle. You are amazing kids!

The "Braverman Four" have always been very close. Our relationship is far from perfect and we each carry our own baggage from the past into the present. We talk frequently and are very open with one another. As close as we are, I could predict the way many of our conversations would go. Mom and Dad, this often made me nervous to call you. I knew your voices and faces would share emotions I just couldn't handle. As a mom myself, I can only imagine what it's like to be on the receiving end of this news about your child.

You recently shared how you felt when I told you I had breast cancer. To know that you were in this state of limbo, of helplessness, during the six weeks before you came to Virginia absolutely breaks my heart. I know you wanted to be with me, to help in any way possible, and I also know I needed time and space to process everything first. I know there were times I was short with you, like when you wanted to know all the info after a doctor's appointment. I simply didn't have the energy, and I appreciate that you tried to understand this. I look back now and know you were trying to fill the distance between us, both figuratively and literally. You couldn't do anything to help me at that time and I am sure that was agonizing.

The moment you arrived in my driveway is a memory that will never fade. The smiles and the tears. A true bittersweet moment for all of us. I don't know what I would do if ever in your situation, and I hope I never have to, but you went above and beyond. The length of time you stayed to help our family, to help me. The emotional support you provided me and continue to provide. The endless loads of laundry, dishes, and grocery shopping you did. For fifteen months, you dropped so much of your life to put my family and me first. I hope you know how much I appreciate and love you both.

Leigh, my sister, my best friend. It wasn't until near the end of treatment that I caught a glimpse of how this had impacted you. You've shielded me from your innermost feelings. You've hidden your fears. You selflessly did this to protect me, so I could focus solely on my healing. You sat with me and comforted me during chemo and as I recovered from surgery. You walked with me, talked, and listened when I needed it most. You allowed me to vent, cry, scream, and, most of all, you taught me that I need to feel all my emotions. I am certain it was hard and I appreciate what you did for me. I pray I am never in your role, and if I am, I vow to be as supportive as you have been for me. I love you more than words can ever express, Leigh.

Thank you all for everything you did for me and for each other. Breast cancer will forever be a part of our story. I am beyond blessed for your love and support, through not only this cancer fuckery but also through all of life.

Love,
Amy

ACKNOWLEDGMENTS

Many people think writing a book looks like an author sitting in a cottage on the beach or in the mountains, with no distractions and no help. This has not been my experience. This book was written in my bed, at my kitchen table, at the library, and at numerous coffee shops. And bringing it to life was not a solo experience.

To my RAW sisters and my girls Courtney, Jen, Lauren, and Layton: Thank you for listening to me talk about this book all the time and for encouraging me when I would question myself or my story.

To Jade and Alisha: Thank you for being brave and honest beta readers of version one. Without your suggestions, this book would not exist in the form it does today. More than anything, thank you for your wisdom, guidance, and love always.

To Lauren and Tina: Thank you for spending many hours as my beta readers and counsel for this book. Your time, energy, and honesty have helped make this book what it is.

To Eric Koester and The Creator Institute: Thank you for providing the structure and deadlines I needed to make this happen.

To everyone I worked with at New Degree Press: Thank you for keeping me in check, catching my errors, and providing guidance to help make sure this would be the best it could possibly be.

To Allie: Thank you for being my writing partner, accountability partner, friend, and kick in the ass when I needed it. Your friendship has been one of the greatest gifts to come out of this book writing process.

To all the doctors, nurses, and techs who were/are part of my cancer treatment team: Thank you for listening to me cry and trying to understand. Thank you for helping me become cancer-free. Thank you for all you do to help those with cancer.

To all those who helped my family and me, who brought us meals, sent flowers, cards, notes, and words of advice, who sat with me at chemo, and who listened to me cry and gave me reasons to keep going—I am forever grateful!

To Tess: Thank you for all the cuddles, snuggles, and comfort you provided me during the fuckery. Thank you for curling up next to me every time I sat down on the couch to write this book.

To Natalie: Thank you for suggesting my haircutting party, for making sure I was comfortable through it all, and for always making me feel beautiful. I can't wait to sit in your chair again with my long, curly locks! Get ready to have some fun!

To Carmel: Thank you for the selfless gift of your home. You will never know how this gesture made life so much easier for my parents, my family, and me during an incredibly difficult time.

To my mom and dad: Thank you for everything, from my birth, until now, and into the future. I am so lucky to have two parents who love me no matter what and support my goals and dreams.

To my sister Leigh: Thank you for knowing I'd write this book before I even knew it, for helping me realize I don't have to be happy and positive all the damn time, for letting me say "fuck" as many times as needed, and for holding my hand, letting me cry, and always meeting for coffee or a walk when I call. I am really fucking lucky to have you as my sister and my best friend.

To Andrew, Jacob, and Zachary: Thank you for understanding when I had to write instead of do something you were asking of me, for being such incredible humans, for always loving me, and for being my motivation in writing this book. I hope it is something you can be proud to say your mom accomplished and that you will share my story with future generations.

To Derek: The cute boy on the other end of the America Online chat room. Cancer was most certainly never in our plans and through it all you showed up big time for me and the boys. Thank you for supporting me endlessly while writing this book and in all my endeavors. Thank you for the time you spent designing and perfecting my book cover. Thank you for doing this thing called life with me and doing the work with me to make our family the best it can be.

To everyone who believed in me and in this book before it was even a book: Your support through my Indiegogo campaign helped make it all a reality. Thank you to my early supporters:

Anne Cassity	Charlotte Hall
Alicia Levy	Chris Larson
Alisha Wielfaert	Christy Lingo
Allison Plessinger	Christian Schoener
Allan & Barbara Ratner	Claudia Schoener
Allison Harvey Griffin	Connie Polito Deam
Allison Prell	Courtney Fox
Amalia Natalio	Courtney Nein
Amanda Edwards	Dana Kornfeld
Andrea Noordyk	Daniela Waters
Andrew Muhl	Deanna Kennedy
Azalea Yow	Debbie Cassell
Barbara & Dennis Consalvo	Debora Morandi
Barbara Knisely Michelman	Debra Purrington
Becky Benak	Debra Silver
Beth & Sheldon Weinberg	Dede Nuckols
Beth Gruber	Dene Sebastiana
Beth Zweig	Denise Develin
Betsy Yakes	Denise Doss
Bobbi Olson	Derek Banocy
Bridget Cavanaugh	Diane Davidson Ozure
Brigid Diehl Cianfrani	Dianne Kotasenski
Bryna Smith	Donna McCaw
Caren Silverman	Dorothy & John Banocy
Carol Wright Fritz	Eileen Castro
Caroline Sprinkel	Elisabeth Pinsky
Catharine Boucher	Elizabeth Fischer
Chandni Saxena	Elizabeth Hunt

Elizabeth Miller
Elizabeth Summers
Elizabeth Walenga
Ellen Kaiden
Eric Koester
Erica Cohen
Erin M. Johnson
Fern G. Skelly
Geoffrey Rowland
Gloria Calloway
Gretchen Wade
Ingre Stackhouse
Jade Eby
Jamie Petersen
Jane Rothman
Janele Marie Marquez
Janet & Stephen Braverman
Janice Lubin Kirschner
Jayne Dunnum
Jen Griswold
Jenna Flynt
Jennifer Barton-McAuliffe
Jennifer Gurley
Jennifer Peatman
Jennifer Rubal
Jeremy Ratner
Jessica Williams
Jill Blackman
Jodi Romano
Jodi Ward
Joel Braverman
Joshua Brockman

Judy & Mat Gluckson
Judy Rothenberg
Judy Wolfberg
Kali Schwindt
Karen Forman
Karen Rusciano
Karen & Marvin Singer
Karen Weinberg
Kate Johns
Kate Schneider
Katie Jefcoat
Ken Ettinger
Kendall Carriere
Kerry-Ann McDonald
Kimberly Ayars
Kristen Nicklas
Kristin Vancleave Smith
Laureen Guerriero
Laurel Rosen
Lauren Bartleson
Lauren DiTullio
Lauren Myers
Laurie Augustino
Laurie Korn
Layton Griffin
Leigh & Eric Schoener
Leslie Wallace
Libby Martin
Lillian Sharlet
Linda Djupstrom
Lisa Carnell
Lisa & Marco Girao

Lisa N. Kritz
Lois Spritzler
Luanne Engh
Mandy Nankivel
Margie Sussman
Margo Guarinello
Marisa Roinestad
Maureen Banocy
Mary Medawar
Melissa de Beer
Melissa Myers
Michelle Dunne
Miles Spence Koerner
Morgan Ohara
Nancy Gutierrez
Nancy Larson
Nancy Roche
Nancy Schachter
Naomi Lewis
Natalie Haar
Nicole Boomgaarden
Niki Cobb
Norman Reich
Patricia Mitchell
Rebecca Aydelette
Rebecca Romary
Rebecca Mann
Robert Feld
Romi Neustadt
Russell Rosen

Ruth Auerbach
Sabine Aldama
Sabine Robinson
Sally Gummel
Sally Spivack
Sara Wall
Sean Boland
Sharon Larson
Sheila Nagorny
Shelisa Welde
Sheryl Klein
Shirley Fajga
Staci & Aleks Dubovik
Stacie McClintock
Stephanie Baer
Susan & Jerry Hale
Susan E. Hildebrand
Susan Spellman
Susie LaCava
Tawnya Baird
Terry Ruby
Ti Stoneman
Tina Yalen
Tamara J. Oster
Tracie Cleek
Tracy Burger
Tracy Steffek
Vera Ventura
Wendy Macaluso
Wendy Silverman

Finally, to anyone I may have left off this list in error: Please know it was just that, a human error, and I blame it on chemo brain.

I love you all deeply!

APPENDIX

AUTHOR'S NOTE

National Breast Cancer Foundation, Inc. 2022. "Breast Cancer Facts." National Breast Cancer Foundation, Inc. Accessed September 2, 2022. https://www.nationalbreastcancer.org/breast-cancer-facts.

RADIATION: THE TECHNICAL SHIT

The Peter MacCallum Cancer Centre. "Deep Inspiration Breath Hold (DIBH)." Peter Mac. Accessed October 4, 2022. https://www.petermac.org/DIBH.

THE EMOTIONAL BURNS

Lowney, Declan, director. 2020. "Make Rebecca Great Again." *Ted Lasso*. AppleTV+. 32 min. https://tv.apple.com/us/episode/make-rebecca-great-again/umc.cmc.1zzkhptbom1da61ga7ars15my?action=play.

FORGED BY FIRE

Richman-Abdou, Kelly. 2022. "Kintsugi: The Centuries-Old Art of Repairing Broken Pottery with Gold." *Art History* (blog), *My Modern Met*. March 5, 2022. https://mymodernmet.com/kintsugi-kintsukuroi/.